120 Ways
To
Attract
The Right
Career
Or
Business

Tried and True

Tips and Techniques

Sue Ellson

Published by
120 Ways Publishing PO Box 65, Surrey Hills, Victoria, Australia, 3127
120ways@120ways.com Book: B0001

Printed by
IngramSpark, Unit A1/A3, 7 Janine Street, Scoresby, Victoria, Australia 3179
ingramsparkinternational@ingramcontent.com

Copyright
All text and technical diagrams copyright © Sue Ellson 2016 The moral rights of the author have been asserted. All rights reserved.

Photocopying and reproducing in print or digital format
If recommending the content in this book to friends, family, clients or colleagues, please keep in mind that the original rights belong to the author only. The content has been generously provided and it is only fair that the reward be returned to the author to recover the cost of production, distribution and future editions.

If you wish to reproduce, store or transmit any part of this book, please email the publisher 120ways@120ways.com for written permission rights. All quotations need to be referenced to Sue Ellson.

National Library of Australia Cataloguing-in-Publication entry
Ellson, Sue, 1965 – Author
120 Ways To Attract The Right Career Or Business
Tried And True Tips And Techniques / Sue Ellson
ISBN-10: 0-9942875-3-4 ISBN 13: 978-0-9942875-3-3 (paperback)
Includes index. Books – Business, Books – Self-Help

Please note
All care has been taken in the preparation of this book. The publisher and the author have no liability to any person or entity with respect to any loss or damage alleged to have been caused directly or indirectly by the information contained herein, which was correct at the time of writing, and is based on past experience, but is subject to change. This content has not been approved or endorsed by any social media or online platform provider. Trademark information has been omitted from the main text to assist readability. All trademarked brands are owned by their respective corporations.

DEDICATION

For my children,
Carmen and Peter,
whom I love more
than words can say.

ACKNOWLEDGEMENTS

I have been given the courage to write this book because I have had various people appear in my life as beacons of inspiration and they have believed in me, even when I didn't believe in myself.

I have been blessed by people from across the world who have acknowledged my writing and encouraged me to include more of my own story in my writing. I am essentially a very private person so it has not been easy for me to include my personal information, but I certainly hope that my story can help you.

Individual people have sometimes challenged me unfairly and yet they have always propelled me to a higher level of understanding and awareness. They have taught me to stand up for myself.

I have also discovered that by being more vulnerable, more authentic and more willing to back myself, I have been able to attract exactly the right career and business opportunities aligned with my values and purpose into my life, which is why I want to share these practical tips and techniques with you.

So to both the believers and the blockers, I say thank you!

I would also like to encourage you to let go of any assumptions you may have about why you do not have exactly the right career or business you want right now – because I am here to share at least 120 ways you can attract the right career and business opportunities!

I wish you every success on your journey.

I trust you will enjoy reading this book and please make sure you TAKE ACTION.

You can stay fully updated in relation to this book and the other 120 Ways Publishing publications by joining the 120 Ways Publishing Membership Program at http://120ways.com/members

Contents

Preface xiii

Introduction 1

1. It's All About You 3
1.1 Personal Responsibility 6
1.2 Action Steps 8
1.3 Skills 10
1.4 Techniques 11

2. Past and Present Context 13
2.1 Future Context 16
2.2 Understanding Yourself 19
2.3 Letting Go 21
2.4 Understanding Value 23
2.5 Understanding Needs 25
2.6 Sense Of Self 27
2.7 Sense Of Others 30

3. Selecting The Right Career Or Business 33

4. Choosing What To Do Right Now 37
4.1 Choosing What To Do In The Future 39

5. Capital Raising 41
5.1 Social Capital 41
5.2 Intellectual Capital 44
5.3 Cultural Capital 44
5.4 Financial Capital 45
5.5 Gratitude Or Operating Capital 48
5.6 Relationship Capital 50
5.7 Credibility Capital 51
5.8 Influence Capital 53

6. Action Steps 55
6.1 Research And Select Your Locations 55
6.2 Establish Quality Real Estate 57
6.3 Review And Verify Your Real Estate 59
6.4 Select Your Strategic Activity 60
6.5 Review, Analyze and Improve 62
6.6 Give Feedback, Follow Up, Say Thank You And Smile. 63
6.7 Celebrate, Acknowledge And Learn 65
6.8 Decide What To Do Next 67

7. Career Attraction Tips and Techniques 69
7.1 Immediate Jobs 70
7.2 Survival Jobs And Means To An End Jobs 72
7.3 Aligned Jobs 73
7.4 Next Step Up Jobs 74
7.5 Job Identification Techniques 77
7.6 Job Application Techniques 79
7.7 Job Application Persistence Techniques 82
7.8 Job Interview Techniques 83
7.9 Job Interview Follow Up Techniques 87
7.10 Accepting A Job Offer 88

8. Business Attraction Tips And Techniques 91
8.1 Real Value In Business 91
8.2 Perceived Value In Business 93
8.3 Referral Value In Business 95
8.4 Clarity Value In Business 97
8.5 Reciprocity Value In Business 99
8.6 Uncertainty Value In Business 102
8.7 Pricing Value In Business 103
8.8 Human Value in Business 104
8.9 Asset Value In Business 106
8.10 Investment Value In Business 108

9. Audience Attraction Techniques 111
9.1 Identifying Audience Locations 112
9.2 Arousing Your Target Audience 114
9.3 Discouraging Your Non Target Audience 115
9.4 Re-Attracting Your Target Audience 118

10. Content Attraction Techniques 119
10.1 Content Guidelines 120
10.2 Content Conversions. 123
10.3 Content Reach 124
10.4 Content Sharing 127
10.5 Content Critics 129

11. People Attraction Techniques 133
11.1 People Background Research 135
11.2 Finding The Right People 137
11.3 Building The Relationship 138
11.4 Refining Your People Attraction Techniques 141

12. Platform Attraction Techniques 143
12.1 Completing Your Platform Profile 144
12.2 Maximizing Each Platform 146
12.3 Measuring Your Platform Performance 147
12.4 Platform Power Tools 149
12.5 Game Changers 151

13. Process Attraction Techniques 155
13.1 Finding Advertised Opportunities 155
13.2 Applying For Advertised Opportunities 156
13.3 Passing the Application Process 159
13.4 Starting A Career Or Business Opportunity 161
13.5 Daily Career And Business Strategies 163
13.6 Education And Learning Based Strategies 164
13.7 Proactive Action Strategies 166
13.8 System Based Strategies 170

14. Possibility Attraction Techniques 173
14.1 Traditional Possibility Sources 173
14.2 Contemporary Possibility Sources 174
14.3 Speculative Possibility Sources 176
14.4 Ongoing Possibility Sources 177

15. Brand Development 179
15.1 Building Your Personal Brand 179
15.2 Building Your Business Brand 180
15.3 Personal Brand Builders 181
15.4 Business Brand Builders 183
15.5 Publicity Tactics 184

16. Network Development 187
16.1 Assessing Networks 187
16.2 Creating A Network 189
16.3 How To Network 191
16.4 Developing Your Network 192
16.5 Valuing Your Network 193

17. Website Development 197
17.1 Personal Career Attraction Website 197
17.2 Personal Business Attraction Website 199
17.3 General Website Attraction Techniques 200
17.4 Website Performance Measures 202
17.5 User Experience And Website Feedback 204

18. Overcoming Challenges 207
18.1 Action Planning Sequence 208
18.2 Measuring Results 210
18.3 Personal Blockages 211
18.4 External Blockages 213
18.5 Top 20 Tips And Techniques 215

19. Full List Of 120 Actions	219
20. Bonuses	234
Index	237
Author	255

Preface

'120 Ways To Attract The Right Career Or Business: Tried And True Tips And Techniques' is for:

- defining your highest values and purpose
- clarifying your vision and overcoming your challenges
- building your attraction power, lifetime value and dynamic value
- securing the right career or business opportunities
- developing your presence, brand and networks
- learning, leading and laughing your way to success

It includes information for:

- students, job seekers and career changers
- freelancers, entrepreneurs and business owners
- advisers, consultants and thought leaders
- coaches, trainers and mentors
- anyone who wants to leverage their skills, knowledge and networks

This thorough, practical and detailed guide provides you with the key strategies and techniques, based on your purpose, that you can implement today for your success in the future.

Get started and take action now!

**Special free bonus offers at http://120ways.com/members

Introduction

Are you clear about your values and purpose in life?

    If the answer is yes, well done!

    If the answer is no, don't worry, it will come!

Do you already know how to attract the right career or business?

    If the answer is yes, fantastic, you are about to learn a lot more!

    If the answer is no, I am so happy that you are willing to learn!

'120 Ways To Attract The Right Career Or Business' has been written to help you choose what actions will be useful for attracting the right career or business opportunity – and give you the courage to complete the right steps to achieve results.

So get ready to take action!

1. It's All About You

There are some everyday principles that we need to consider when thinking about attracting the right career or business.

I have worked with hundreds of people to help them find the career or business that they are seeking and I can tell you that the most successful people achieve results through:

- clarity
- authenticity
- persistence
- taking regular, personally selected, action
- sharing consistent messages
- implementing multiple concurrent strategies
- making regular adjustments based on new reliable information, tests and experiments

They also develop particular life strategies that are to be admired. They:

- are prepared to take risks
- seek inspiration whilst they are on the journey
- believe in a fair exchange for everyone (not how to compete or win at all costs)
- are happy now and will also be happy when their goal is reached in the future
- prefer to live with the consequences of a mistake rather than the regret of not taking action
- are willing to say 'no' if necessary or 'yes' if the opportunity is aligned
- start with the most important tasks, realizing that 'done' is better than 'perfect'
- are very willing to learn and regularly seek opportunities to learn more
- can delay instant gratification because they believe that great things can be achieved over time

- create a spiders web to attract opportunities and they have a backup plan as well
- realize that there are many ways to reach a destination
- provide descriptive and positive feedback
- praise others and celebrate achievements
- always say thank you personally

On the journey to success, you will discover that self-discipline takes effort. Would you rather live with the pain of self-regret? Do you want to be the driver on the journey or the passenger in the back seat squashed in between two other people with no room to move?

My goal is to help you move from action to attraction. If you have found your purpose and mission, you can align your life. You can set your intention and get results. You will be successful in your own way and ultimately, have the opportunity to leave a legacy and lead a life full of personal significance.

If you have been seduced into believing that profit is more important than purpose, you run the risk of being perceived as a mercenary rather than a missionary. The currency that has value in every country across the world is trust and it is priceless.

Opportunities can spread like a virus, but needs are often ignored. We can all remember avoiding situations where a person was needy because they were seeking something they didn't have and being attracted to a person who has something to offer.

Luck is a residue of design. It appears when systems and processes have come together in a congruent way. Do not be tempted to judge someone else by the 'luck' they have received. Everyone's journey is unique and some of the 'unluckiest' people in the world are the happiest and most content.

When selecting what you will do from this book, remember that the best resources are usually attracted to the most meaningful work. Think back to when a disaster has occurred in your local area. Did you notice that all of a sudden, people would find the time or money to assist?

Don't waste your time seeking the biggest wins. Aim for some fast wins, often called the 'low hanging fruit.' It is amazing how one small win can lead to another, then another, then another and so on.

For many people, your values will remain fairly consistent throughout your life. To maintain and achieve goals related to those values, you will sometimes need to change your behaviors.

Your current beliefs are based on the descriptions you have attached to your experiences and decisions from your past. If you can change the way you view those decisions, you can change your beliefs about the present.

Let's look at an example. Let's imagine you were at school as a child and the teacher gave you some personal praise for the homework you had completed in front of the whole class. However, you had a friend in the same class whose work you believed was always better than yours – so rather than accept the compliment from the teacher, you dismissed it because of your belief that your friend's homework was always better than yours.

If you revisit this example now as an adult and actually accept that your homework could have been praiseworthy in its own right, then you may also be able to accept praise from other sources and not dismiss it.

I was personally challenged by a very similar experience. For years, even though people would give me praise for my achievements, I would always dismiss it. I would be polite and say thank you but not formally acknowledge it in my own mind. Then one day, I received a compliment from someone whom I personally admired and she is always extremely frank and would never say well done unless something really was well done. This time I could not ignore it. All of a sudden, a terrifying feeling of fear welled up in my stomach.

On the same day, I went to visit a friend who knows me very well and I asked him why I was so scared of receiving a compliment? He told me it was because on this occasion, I couldn't deny the compliment. I knew that she had spoken the truth and what I had done really was terrific. How bizarre!

I wonder, how many of these types of beliefs are you carrying with you? How many beliefs do you have that have been created from incorrect assumptions, one off anecdotes or bad behavior by someone else? If you could re-visit these situations and re-frame what you believe to be true, you may find that your potential really is unlimited!

I believe that loving what you do is the gift of life. That includes the exciting and the mundane. The simple and the complex. The easy and the difficult. Selecting what you do with your time is important. If you are clear about your aspirations, you will find the time to complete the right actions to achieve your goals.

However, getting things done takes an ongoing sequence of steps. The Great Wall of China was built one brick at a time, by many people, a long time ago. It still stands today and it can be seen from space. What a legacy! You can create your own legacy too!!

Action 5: *Write down three beliefs that you have about yourself that are not serving you well. Think about what happened at the time you created those beliefs and re-assess whether or not they are 'true' beliefs or 'circumstantial' beliefs. Now is the time to let go of limiting beliefs and start creating potential beliefs*

_____

_____

_____

1.1 Personal Responsibility

Are you someone who knows what you want but haven't been able to get it? Have you used more than five different strategies on a sustained basis over a period of time to reach your ideal goal? Or are you looking for a silver bullet that will solve your issue in one shot?

Let's start with a dose of reality. We all know about 'get rich quick schemes.' Perhaps we have also heard of 'one hit wonders.' Why do we expect instant gratification for free nowadays? Did Google start this trend?

Let me ask you another tough question. What do you take for free? Do you download free movies or music? Do you take supplies from your workplace for your personal use? Do you choose not to return an oversupply of cash change you receive? Do you sneak an extra refreshment from a buffet table for consumption after the meal time? Unfortunately, I must admit, I have done all of these things in the past…but I have made a conscious decision not to do them in the future.

My children chose to buy me a new bread toaster and they were able to purchase it for just $7. On the one hand, I admire their budgeting skills and the ability to shop around for a cheaper price. The normal price, even for the most basic toaster at most shops, would normally be at least $25. I have to wonder whose lifestyle has been sacrificed so that in my country, I can access such cheap products. The toaster lasted two months before it blew up and was useless. Conversely, the toaster my sister gave me 10 years prior was still functional when I sent it off for recycling (even though some parts of the elements weren't working).

I do understand that the overall level of opportunity for most of the population of the world has increased thanks to large scale manufacturing and technological design improvements. I am also aware that an enormous amount of this manufacturing is completed in countries with low wages by the living poor. I am not saying that the people who purchase these cheap items are doing the wrong thing (sometimes, no other products are available). I also know that too few people in the world have most of the money (this is a tragedy). I guess I just wonder if we were all willing to 'pay our share,' whether or not all of our societies would be more equitable and give everyone an opportunity to attract the right career or business for their unique capabilities? I would also like a toaster that lasts longer than two months and doesn't end up in landfill!

I do not want you to take any offence from these statements. My goal is to help you recognize the best ways to move towards the career or business you are seeking. I want to help you do this with a realistic and optimistic approach. I want to empower you with the internal motivation to move towards your goal in what may sometimes appear to be a constantly changing and hostile environment with a lot of cheap competition.

I have managed to stop my 'free-loading' by thinking about the concept of a 'fair exchange.' When all is said and done, I really appreciate the people who go to all of the expense, time and effort to create a movie and I am happy to pay $7 for the privilege of watching their work in the comfort of my own home. In turn, if someone wants to utilize my expertise, I would like to receive a return. It doesn't necessarily need to be money, but there does need to be a fair exchange.

Please do not be too proud if you find yourself in a situation where you need to access free or low cost services. These services have been developed to provide a safety net in times of need, so allow others to give you a hand up (not a hand out). When you receive this gift, work out ways that you can potentially return the benefit – to either the giver or someone else who needs help now or in the future – it could be a simple as spending some time with someone who is lonely – that gift is priceless. You will also feel as if you are giving a fair exchange in return for the benefit you are receiving.

I did this when I was receiving a welfare payment when my children were young and I could not access childcare. In return for the 'benefit' I received from the government, I regularly volunteered for community organizations. That way, I did not feel as if I was using anyone else, I was still 'working' for my payment.

Action 6: *Accept full responsibility for all of your actions and always operate on the basis of a fair exchange – pay for a benefit you receive and reward the creator so that you in turn can be rewarded for your efforts*

1.2 Action Steps

The next step to overcome for most people is procrastination. This is the enemy of opportunity. Attracting the right career or business takes action, not wishing. Clever action, aligned with your goals. The best way to overcome procrastination for me is to do something, even if I do not feel like doing the original task I have set myself.

I spent nearly 10 years in what I call the wilderness. Where I would get up each morning and try and move towards my goals and dreams, but often be incapable of moving as quickly and as easily as I would like.

So I had to learn more about myself and how I could move forward in a way that worked for me. What I worked out was that although I may have chosen to do a particular task on a particular day, quite often, at that moment, I was unable to do it. Usually because my brain was 'foggy.' Unfortunately, I couldn't even force myself to do it.

Rather than wallow in this situation, I worked out that doing something rather than nothing was a step forward. So I would do any task rather than no task. Even something as simple as housework. Interestingly, that would often switch my brain over and I was then able to start the task I had previously found difficult.

A lot of people have told me I should write things down. So I started writing to-do lists and I would become even more frustrated because then there was even more that I 'needed to do' and so much I still couldn't get done. I still have a huge list of items on those lists stored safely in a folder in a cupboard.

If I had stuck to those lists, I wouldn't be writing this book! (What I have since learnt is to put what I want to get done on a to-do schedule. So when I decided I wanted to write and publish a book, I set the date for a book launch – that way, I had to get the task completed so that there was a book to launch!)

Anyway, during my wilderness stage, I eventually completed the initial tasks on a very gradual basis but I still had an overwhelming sense of isolation and disappointment when I realized that I still wasn't really moving towards my ultimate goals. I knew what I needed to do (I have certainly attended plenty of courses, conferences, seminars, workshops, events and coaching sessions to know the steps), but I wasn't getting it done. I needed to be made accountable for my actions.

So I found my own Accountability Partner. We met once a week for one hour in person and spent half an hour each sharing our achievements, challenges and plans. This set in motion the next step.

More useful and productive action. I realized that if I was really serious about changing my circumstances, I had to change my environment and my habits. I hired a university student on a part time basis and I went through the process of 'cleaning up my mess.' Sorting files, clearing clutter and re-organizing my life. This process is still continuing and will for some time yet.

What was most interesting about this process was the fact that I was able to let go of old habits, incomplete projects and objects I really did not need to keep (and I have willingly given those items to people who can use them). If I was really serious about moving forward, I had to make room for the new things to come into my life.

I went to a seminar more recently and was told that the people who are not achieving their goals are the 'victims' of our society. The people who blame other people and circumstances for their present situation and are firmly stuck on one way being the only way out (and they will often defend that reason based on their view of the world – for example, all the jobs are going to younger people and they are not young).

I am not here to blame anyone for anything. I want to show the way forward based on a lot of tried and true tips and techniques. If you want to beat procrastination, work out what techniques will help you beat it! After you have jumped the first hurdle, the rest will become easier.

Action 7: *Identify the three best ways to make sure you complete the actions you choose to do in the future, remembering that unless you have absolute clarity, your chances of conversion will be limited*

_____

_____

_____

1.3 Skills

My brother started his working life in the navy. Despite learning how to sail at the age of 15, I have to say that tying knots has never been my strength. Sure, I can do a reef knot, a figure of eight knot and even a bow line, but ask me to do a clove hitch or a slip knot and I get confused every time.

My brother once told me that his supervisor in the navy told him 'if you can't tie knots, tie lots.' I love this metaphor.

We don't necessarily need to know the one silver bullet based on knowledge, skills or experience to solve a problem instantly. The reality is that people who can solve issues instantly have usually earned the ability to do so – they can tie the best knot for the situation immediately because they have acquired those skills over time.

For most of us, we start with a few knots (skills) and we keep using those skills (knot types) until we get what we want (a knot that holds items securely).

As a 'learning junkie,' I have attended a huge range of seminars over many years (to this day, I usually go to between one and four events per week). The presenters have usually spent several years learning their 'knots' and they usually present their offerings (products and services) as the silver bullet that you need to use or purchase to solve your problem.

I have seen scores of attendees rush to the back of the room to pay money for the showcased program (often more than $4,000) at the end of the presentation and then they go home and do not implement the system and don't achieve their goals. They needed to take action and follow through.

My suggestion is to constantly learn new skills, constantly develop those skills with experience and be prudent before selecting 'quick fix' options. If you have to learn whilst you are 'on the job,' that is okay. Some of the most successful start-ups have started with zero funds and grown organically without a funds injection from a venture capitalist. These people have learnt along on the way. Taking action, taking calculated risks, learning by mistake, but definitely moving forward (and not at someone else's expense either).

Action 8: *Be prepared to learn new skills through formal and informal training for the rest of your life. Don't be worried about making mistakes, especially if you are taking calculated risks – just keep taking action*

1.4 Techniques

Starting with a personal responsibility review and first steps leads to taking some action. That leads to taking more targeted effective action and letting go of ideas and items from your past. Then comes accountability and skills that can genuinely move you in the right direction.

What are the techniques you need to implement to move forward? One thing I know for sure is that you need to allocate regular time and effort. If it is your main priority, I usually suggest two hours per day, five days per week.

The rest of this book will talk about the different types of techniques you can choose for your purpose. When selecting what you will do, please consider the following overall techniques:

- choose some easy options as a starting point
- choose some concepts that challenge you
- find people who can encourage you (not criticize you)
- find people and services that can help you (including paid, professional help)
- select individual tasks and select realistic dates for them to be completed
- keep records so that you can track what is working well and what can be changed or stopped
- review your progress regularly so that you can 'sharpen the saw' rather than try cutting down the tree for hours with a blunt saw

Action 9: *Selecting and completing a variety of actions that are both easy and challenging will lead you to results. Find people and services that can help you on your journey*

2. Past and Present Context

The first part of this book has really focused on you as an individual and has looked at some of the triggers in your life that have brought you to the present moment. Your peers, friends and family have been a significant influence on your life.

The ability to move forward in life is based on your ability to learn, unlearn and relearn so that you can transfer knowledge into wisdom.

You will also be aware by now that there is no quick fix and the process will involve many stages. One of the biggest challenges is not to come up with new ideas but to let go of old ideas.

You may have also realized that the traditional teaching environment in schools involves you working on your own for a large percentage of the time, to request permission to speak (by raising your hand) and to ask before you receive.

Paradoxically, if you would like to move into the world of attraction, you need to learn to give rather than to receive. The best news is that there is usually a limit of what you can 'get' in life, but there is usually no limit on what you can 'give.'

Traditional careers in the recent past were usually very specific roles within organizations. The world is changing so rapidly now that any concept of what is normal is very quickly replaced by the 'new normal.'

This means that rather than think of the skills you have and how they can match certain jobs or enterprises, you need to think about the value you offer and how you can make a contribution to a job or an enterprise. You also need to be proactive about ensuring that the enterprise remains viable by being willing to provide feedback and insights whilst you are in a role.

This also means that our career pathways need to be more personalized than ever before. Gone are the days when women were either secretaries, nurses or teachers and only able to work until they got married. The average duration of a job has dropped from seven years to just three or four years.

Younger generations are coming to the workforce with very different expectations and many are more focused on working to live rather than living to work. A lower birth rate in many countries requires people to have more adaptable skills throughout their working career – especially when most businesses only last five to seven years. Older workers are choosing 'protirement' (professional retirement) rather than 'retirement' so that they can continue to utilize their skills and talents in a more gentle transition to old age.

In a world that is constantly adjusting to technology and the replacement of many roles through some form of automation or aggregation, success is now dependent upon non-cognitive skills. Your ability to interact socially, build rapport, to do the hard work, utilize your experience, persevere in difficult times and have patience and conviction that everything will be okay are essential skills for living in modern society.

The new currency, as mentioned previously, is trust. If a promise is made and it is delivered, trust is earned. Good quality unique content (via online or offline methods) increases the awareness of a brand and that increases sales. But finding a way to inspire and educate consumers in a cluttered world is becoming increasingly difficult.

Consumers are still responding to benefits described in an emotive or experiential manner rather than in a rational manner focusing on features. However, if they are looking for particular features and these cannot be found with the details of the product or service, consumers will go where they can find the details they are seeking (so businesses must think of the customer experience at all times).

An example of this is cars. A car manufacturer may have a very fancy website that allows you to select the color or make and model of the car you like and make the screen change in front of your eyes so you can see how the care will look, but if you want to purchase the car to tow a trailer or a caravan and it doesn't include the towing capacity of the various cars, you are likely to look at a different car manufacturer that does supply the towing capacity information.

There is another force that is also affecting everyday life – the collective unconscious. As more and more content is personalized for the individual based on their personal behavior, people connected to the digital world are becoming increasingly self-determining and self-selecting (or predictively encouraged) and this can easily bypass the opportunity for individuals to develop a range of general knowledge. For some people, this creates a level of extreme synchronicity and alignment – for others, it creates a desperate sense of isolation and disconnection. I believe that these streams of consciousness are affecting what people value and I also believe, are reducing our ability to empathize and understand our fellow man.

If you have started to consider all of these factors but you have not completed any steps towards your career or business goals, you probably fall into the category of 'over investing and under implementing.' If you are starting to feel as if you have been left behind, you may not be keeping yourself up to date. If you are feeling overwhelmed, you may have jumped a few steps too early and tried to do it all yourself. Alternatively, you may be waiting for all of your 'ducks to line up' or for another solution to appear.

Perhaps you even fear being successful or standing out in front of others? One thing is for sure, the world is changing and it is changing rapidly.

The information you need to find for your purpose could be provided by an expert, but to make the best use of the information, I encourage you to consider professional support and advice so that you can make wise decisions. Successful people know how to find what they are seeking and are able to source and hire the assistance they need. They are not afraid of making a choice – but they do rely on expert advice first. They may pay a premium for this advice (because the expert had to learn it all first), but they save themselves a lot of time and effort as they do not have to learn all the skills first and then do it themselves.

Thanks to both faster travel options and technology, labor is being traded internationally and as so many tasks can now be clearly defined, more and more individual experts and freelancers are specializing in vertical niches. These individuals must still educate themselves adequately and master their skill set. The people who have mastered a range of skills and developed a range of networks that can refer demand to them, these are the people who will remain employable now and in the future. I would suggest that even these people need to spend up to 10% of their time keeping themselves up to date.

Some of the skills you must definitely maintain and improve over time include:

- general knowledge
- digital literacy
- industry or profession accreditation
- professional association membership
- network literacy
- relationship literacy
- empathy and humility

Action 10: *Allocate up to 10% of your time to constantly learn, grow and develop to remain employable both now and in the future*

2.1 Future Context

The rate of change is occurring so fast (doubling every year) that many individuals no longer feel safe and secure in their everyday life. 20% of the internet searches we do every day are brand new searches.

Privacy appears to be vanishing and personal identity is slowly disappearing. Trying to make sense of all of this change or attempting to control the outcomes is essentially futile. As human beings, we need to ensure that our legislators and officials retain ethical and humanitarian standards and as individuals, we need to understand both our rights and our responsibilities.

The economic models are changing too. Some people suggest we are moving towards a:

- **Gig economy** – where people go from gig to gig based on demand rather than job to job

- **Attention economy** – where business needs to successfully attract relevant attention in a noisy environment but not annoyingly disturb someone's everyday routine

- **Reputation economy** – where a reputation needs to be verifiable to secure business

- **Referral economy** – where people are actively sourced through other people
- **Sharing economy** – where individuals can benefit from the combined resources of a group platform
- **Knowledge economy** – where a high level of knowledge and expertise is required to secure business
- **Demand economy** – where supply is based on demand and trends need to be closely monitored
- **Social economy** – where influencers on social media dictate trends and viral content convinces the masses

Most of these models can be summarized by a focus on the individual customer experience. Gone are the days when customers were grouped into demographic categories and targeted accordingly. The huge amount of data, analytics and data science is driving a behavior led business model.

Data algorithms, artificial intelligence and predictive intelligence are being used to monitor customer intent rather than traffic. This high degree of personalization is changing expectations and behaviors and is moving us towards cognitive computing, where both man and machine are working together, collecting relevant data, calculating relevant insights and making decisions.

This complex research provides enterprises with the ability to evaluate the most productive (or profitable) outcomes and then repeat those processes more efficiently and effectively. It enables enterprises to cast a tailored net and fish in the exact spot where the fish are biting.

These new models also enable enterprises to listen in to what consumers say and do. Scanners are monitoring retail traffic and software is tracking mouse movements, voice conversations and text commands. For the moment, these systems are providing trends but not a full analysis (in part due to privacy laws) – but as there are now opt-in 'privacy by choice' systems, consumers who are willing to receive a discount or win a prize are becoming more willing to share the details of their behavior. How consumers will be able to resist this tracking when technology is mostly wearable, I don't know. Advanced apps have the potential to be game changers in the future.

For now, computers are much better calculators than humans. We can also command computers to do what we want by utilizing various types of code. However, what gives me hope for the future is I cannot think of any system that operates as efficiently as a human body. A computer and an algorithm can mimic a great deal of human capacity, but it would take an incredible number of computers to make sense of everything we each learn on a daily basis and our ability to amalgamate and process so many different pieces of information based on cognitive thought, education and experience. The subtleties we have learned through our families and friends will take a huge amount of recording and computation to emulate. That said, I do not doubt the human ability to one day be able to achieve this via a created device.

Most people do not like to be told what to do. For this reason, I am simply going to pose a few questions that may help you reflect on the choices you can make after absorbing this information:

- Do you want to be part of an enterprise that is on the old path or the new path?
- Do you want to face the world with positive optimism or negative pessimism?
- Will you rely on facts and stats or will you seek insight and inspiration from new data?
- Will you be willing to outsource, crowdsource or crowdfund to achieve your goals?
- Will you adopt a local or global perspective to your job or enterprise?
- Will you target the best employers who usually earn four times the profit and generate three times the stock returns because they offer the promise of a brighter future?
- Will you strive for real results rather than vanity statistics, glory or numbers?
- Will you be prepared for the day when your executor needs to close all of your digital identities? (in other words, you need to start keeping your login details now)

We live in a world where the level of complexity appears to be increasing. Keeping up with the facts is virtually impossible. In my view, we need to work out how to be clear on our values, purpose and priorities. This will give us a simple framework for making aligned choices. We may need coaching and support to come to the right conclusions, but what we must not do is just bury our head in the sand and hope it all goes away. It won't.

Action 11: *Ask yourself how you will set the framework for your future decision making in an uncertain environment. Decide whether or not you need some coaching assistance to create your personal model for the future*

2.2 Understanding Yourself

If you know yourself, you can work out your options, make decisions and build and manage your future. Trust allows attraction to occur. Internal trust will give you confidence. External trust will give you credibility.

By adopting an attitude of responsibility for your life, you will be able to control your life direction. Having a clear vision makes things happen. The greater your desire, the greater is your probability of success. Did you know that the brain cannot tell the difference between what is real and what is imagined? Is it any wonder we find children who are able to 'spend time with the fairies' in a fantasy world of their own creation? Or that the most successful people will say 'I visualized it first.'

Most people feel fear because of the unknown. What could, would or should happen at some point in the future? In this state, it is easy to become paralyzed and not move forward. Whilst you may have a rational mind and be able to complete certain actions, it is usually your emotions that are the driver for your actions. Understanding this will help you realize that you really need to understand how you are feeling, because bad feelings have the opportunity to sabotage your efforts before you begin.

Which of the following applies to you? Do you:

- avoid pain or move toward pleasure?
- have limited resources or limited resourcefulness?
- seek inspiration or react to disappointment?
- desire money or meaningful purpose?
- have a fixed mindset or a growth mindset?

- ask yourself the tough questions or ignore reality?
- constantly analyze rather than strategize?
- turn down the wrong opportunity so you can keep taking steps towards the right opportunity?
- focus on providing value to others by learning transferable skills or rely on existing skills learnt in the past?
- know what your values are and what motivates you?
- celebrate your wins?
- acknowledge what you have accomplished even if it didn't lead to the outcome you wanted?
- identify and respond to your failures?
- pay yourself first or spend first?
- save a percentage of your income at all times?
- proactively go with the flow or fight the current?

Please do not be too disappointed at this point if you realize that there are a lot of things on this list you need to change to attract the opportunity you want in the future. The discipline of taking small steps in the right direction will lead to an increase in your self-commitment and an increase in your self-worth – which means that it will get easier once you get started!

Changing your overall attitude to life will give you a new perspective. It will help you adjust your mindset and help you realize what is possible. You will then find it easier to determine what you need to do and how you can go about it. Your standards, what you choose to accept or settle for have led you to this point in your life. Higher standards can help you achieve your goals.

You may know that depression is usually associated with attachments to what has happened in the past and that anxiety is associated with concerns about the future. If you need help to move along to the next level of your development, you will probably need to source some assistance from someone who has already reached the next level of development or consciousness. They have usually been on your path and been prepared to be vulnerable in the eyes of someone else because they have decided it is more important to be themselves and move forward than it is to conform to what their peers expect. They have discovered the bliss and the power that exists when you choose to be you.

Most people only get to this point when they reach old age and realize that so much of what they thought matters, doesn't matter. They become comfortable with being authentic (and perhaps also a little grumpy). The people I admire most in the world are those who have the courage to be themselves (but they are still courteous and respectful to others). Their zest for life and their example of authenticity is both inspiring and contagious!

Action 12: *Write down three things you could realistically achieve in the next three months. Visualize yourself after you have completed each of these tasks. Imagine the smile on your face, the feeling inside your body and where you will be. Make it feel as real as possible and then write down how you will celebrate each of those achievements*

_____

_____

_____

2.3 Letting Go

Did you know that your career or business can be the path to your recovery? I have personally seen people recover from traumatic relationship breakdowns thanks to the consistency of their employment and the love and respect they regularly received from their colleagues. I have watched people's level of happiness soar once they find their true vocation and change their career. I have celebrated with people who have not only changed their life direction but then modified it afterwards to a new and higher level because they no longer have the inner sabotaging monologue of their parents or anyone else holding them back.

Please remember that anecdotes are just anecdotes. If something happens once, it doesn't mean that it will happen over and over again for the rest of your life. It may have been particularly traumatic, but I know that you can, in time, overcome it. You will be able to overcome it even faster if you adopt the right strategies.

Start by applying the ACT principle. Action Changes Things. In my personal view, action is the only thing that changes things. It can be as simple as changing a thought or it could be repeating something 1,000 times over for two years to create a new neural pathway. Opportunity changes over time. What you have seen cannot be unseen. Fortunately, how you process that experience can be changed.

Several years ago, I was confronted with a very traumatic event associated with one of my relatives. It took me to a place where I was literally unable to function beyond getting up, making meals and going to bed. I was in a horrendous daze and had an uncontrollable and overwhelming feeling of guilt even though I was not responsible for what had happened. I will not reveal what happened out of respect for my relative. Suffice to say that it was impossible for me to get out of this dark place without professional assistance.

On this particular occasion, I went to see a hypnotherapist. To my complete and utter surprise, I was able to release this major issue in one session. I was dumbfounded. It did not change the situation. It did not remove it from my memory. I still feel a sense of sadness and disappointment when I think about what happened. But it no longer paralyzes me. It does not stop me from experiencing joy and moving on with my life.

I should also add that over the years, I have seen a huge range of health and development professionals to move myself past the challenges I have faced. Whilst the hypnotherapist helped me move past this one particular issue, he was unable to help me move past other challenges. So that is when I moved on to the next person who could take me to the next level. And so the journey continues.

Each of the people assisting me on my path have been at least one level above me. When I reach that level, I need to let go of them to maintain the flow in my life. The pain is always greater if I choose to stay at a certain level. I also believe we are genetically programmed to keep growing.

Action 13: *Write down one thing that you need to let go of to move forward in your life. Be as descriptive as possible – what, how, when, where, why and with who it happened. Then work out what type of professional could help you let go of this issue. Find this professional and make an appointment to see them*

2.4 Understanding Value

Have you ever noticed how the people who appear to have a lot of success are usually pursuing a worthy cause or belief? Have you noticed how many financially successful people also align themselves with a charity, welfare or social enterprise?

Did you also know that the more you value yourself, the more worth you will attract? This is probably the most important point in the whole book. I will repeat it.

THE MORE YOU VALUE YOURSELF, THE MORE WORTH YOU WILL ATTRACT.

This doesn't necessarily mean financial wealth. I believe that the greatest worth I have in my life is the relationship I have with my children. If I cannot value myself and our relationship, they will not value themselves and our relationship.

If you have ever been on an aircraft and listened to the safety demonstration, they will tell you that in the event of an emergency, you must fit the oxygen mask to yourself before you assist anyone else. You need to look after yourself so that you can look after others.

The second highest worth I have is my physical health. I am truly blessed to have excellent physical health and I do my level best to maintain it within the demands of my life. I have had challenges with my mental health and I believe that true freedom can be found when we can make sense of ourselves and our surroundings – so this is an area of my life that allows me to constantly grow and develop.

Financial wealth is something that has alluded me for most of my life. On the one hand, this has created challenges of its own. On the other hand, it has been the greatest gift because it has allowed me to focus on my purpose which means that I do not live with any regrets. In my mind, no amount of money could replace the value I have gained from living a life of purpose. What has also helped is that I have also developed the ability to enjoy the simplest things in life. Clean sheets and fresh towels. Sun on a cold day and wind in my hair. A meaningful conversation and the touch of a hand. Chocolate. Dark Chocolate. I could go on but you might start getting hungry…

There is a fabulous expression that really resonates with me. Some people know the price of everything, and the value of nothing. I encourage you not to look at the price of what you desire, but see the value of what you already have.

I am not suggesting that you should do everything just for yourself and not for others. Part of the value you have could be the people around you. I am simply suggesting that you value yourself as well as value others if you want to live a life based on attracting the right career or business.

I also believe you need to give before expecting to receive. So many people in business fail because they ask for a return too quickly and don't provide enough value upfront. They expect to spend $1 and earn $2, from day one.

Some of the most successful businesses in the world operate on a margin of just 5%. That means that the cost of the goods sold is 95 cents for every $1 of revenue. This business model is very finely tuned and to remain viable, the organization needs to constantly monitor and measure their performance and make corrections along the way. A 5% margin is extremely small – but if they can also build in scale (multiple standard replications), they can leverage that 5% and continue to grow. The consumer also wins because they are getting 95 cents of value for every $1 they spend. This is also a fair exchange.

If you think about artists, writers, musicians and creators, they do everything up front and then rely on someone paying them for the work after it has been done. They give 100% up front and hope that someone gives them something in return. That is a huge risk – and you may wonder why they would even consider it! If what they have created gives you value, why wouldn't you pay a reasonable amount for it?

A doer is someone who looks at the detail and asks why they have to do something. A creator asks what's important and then does it. If you are going to live a life of purpose based on your values, a creator mindset will allow you to focus on what is important rather than just what could be done.

Action 14: *Write down the number one thing in your life that you value more than anything else. Describe the value that it gives you and how it adds meaning and purpose to your life*

_____

_____

_____

2.5 Understanding Needs

All of us have both intrinsic needs and extrinsic needs. If you are selecting a career or business based on your purpose where you receive both fulfilment and inspiration you are likely to stay in it.

If you choose a role based on people where you receive both engagement and perks, you may stay in it.

However, if you choose a role based purely on profit where you receive professional development and an income, you are not likely to stay in it, at least not for the long term.

One of the most well-known reasons as to why people leave a job is because they do not get on with the other people they work with and that person is usually their manager. Most of us want a level of autonomy and we would like to feel as if we are in flow. We need to have a level of competence to be able to do our tasks and we can be compelled to contribute if we have a sense of relatedness to our role.

To be able to complete tasks in a career, you need to know what to do, you need to have the materials to do it, you need to have an opportunity to do it, you need to have a supervisor or colleague who cares about your contribution and you need to know that your opinions count. If you are in a job now and more than one of these areas is not working well for you, it is fairly likely that you are considering different options in the future.

Which of the following are your greatest needs?

- certainty
- uncertainty
- variety
- routine
- significance
- success
- security
- connection / love
- growth / learning
- contribution / giving
- challenge
- simplicity
- _____

For the effort you give, what is the measure you have for assessing your return on investment? Financial reward, happiness, synchronicity, recognition, power, performance or something else?

The strength of your character will determine the direction you take and the attitude you have along the way. You may have been driven by money in the past and come to a point in your life where other things are now more important. Alternatively, you may have been extremely poor and now you see financial success as a way to alleviate your struggles.

Understanding the underlying needs you have, the subconscious aspects of your personality based on your previous experiences and interpretations of those experiences will help you understand the emotional drivers determining your actions.

Whilst you may think that your values and purpose are the most important determinants of your future, if you have not had your underlying needs met it could mean that you are unconsciously trying to get these needs met first (and sabotaging your own efforts). Recognizing these needs could help you satisfy that hunger and let you move beyond it – just like limiting beliefs can stop you from having the courage to live according to your values.

For example, you may have been working really hard towards a goal and everybody keeps telling you it is a waste of time. What you really want is someone to recognize your efforts and believe in your idea. So whilst you value a reward, your need right now is to be recognized. You may continue to seek that recognition even when what you absolutely need to survive is a reward. If you can find a way to have that subconscious need for recognition met, you will then be able to look at the situation more clearly, correct your actions and align them with your values and be rewarded for your efforts.

The best example of this is the family member who wants to be writer and everyone else just tells him to 'get a real job' so he can pay his bills. He sabotages his own efforts to make money writing (for example, he doesn't apply for a copywriting job) but he continues writing what he wants to write most of the time and living week to week with casual jobs he hates.

Action 15: *Look at your life right now and identify any subconscious needs that could be interfering with your values and your ability to align your actions with your purpose. Write them down and work out how you will get these needs met so that you can move towards your true values and purpose*

_____

_____

_____

2.6 Sense Of Self

If everything at the moment feels like it is hard work, you are probably doing the wrong thing. If you are constantly tired and drained and feeling worn out, you are not living a life of purpose. What is even worse is that you will not attract what you want either.

When you live through your heart, you will be responding to emotions and following them. When you live through your gut, you will be trusting your instinct and acting accordingly. When you live through your brain, you can plan and be rational.

Rather than coming to the conclusion of 'why,' try coming to the conclusion of 'how.' What skills do you have that you can develop? If you clarify your values and do the necessary research to source realistic solutions, you can attract the right career or business.

Most of us develop our sense of self from the people around us. These people mirror our self-image and give us feedback about how we appear in their eyes (e.g. you are the 'academic/artist/businessperson' of the family). When you leave your friends and family behind and move to a new location, you are likely to feel a huge sense of loss because that mirror disappears. If you think about your life right now and the people you interact with, what do they reflect to you?

Do they tell you that you are smart, capable and inspiring? Or do they suggest that you are lazy, weird and boring? Are you aware of the cultural norms and preferences of the tribes you live in – at home, at work and in your social life? Which of the following intelligences have you developed?

- emotional intelligence
- intellectual intelligence
- cultural intelligence
- skills intelligence

Are you rigid and defined or flexible and adaptable? Have you acknowledged your skills, experience, education and achievements or do you brush these aside and look at what is wrong with you rather than what is right? Do you rely on your brains or your brawn (physical strength)? Are you a doing person or a being person? Are you a one stop wonder or a destination worth reaching? Do you focus on what you do best and outsource the rest?

Do you measure what you have done rather than what you have to do? A healthy balance of both is important for moving forward.

Are you curious about learning more or are you resting on your past credentials? The number one currency is trust – and the number one asset is loyalty. Are you being loyal to yourself to make sure that you keep achieving your goals? Do you give your loyalty away to others instead? I encourage you to have loyalty to yourself and to others.

What is your unique selling proposition? The greatest value that you can bring to your career or business? If you are clear about this, you won't be worried about other people who have similar skill sets, you will be clear in your own mind of the intrinsic value you bring and you will be willing to share it. You will be able to clearly describe your value and not be worried about competition.

For example, I am now writing my second book. There are plenty of people who have written books on both careers and business in the past and they too have an important message (I know, I have read several books about careers and business!). That doesn't mean that what I have to share is not worth writing. It simply means that what I have written is suitable for a slightly different audience (or perhaps the same audience who wants to learn more). I defy anyone to automatically come up with the same content that is in this book without ever reading it! Likewise, there is nobody on this planet that is the same as you! Similar perhaps, but never the same.

The merit you are recognized for is based on both your performance and your potential. If you are aiming to attract the right career or business, you need to demonstrate how your potential will always increase rather than remain static.

A strong sense of self comes with both power and responsibility. You need to be willing to own it and use it for the greater good. It will give you the opportunity to learn and make decisions for yourself that will last. To exist in a world that is changing so rapidly, you need to attract aligned opportunities.

In my view, the level of ambition you have towards your clearly defined goals will determine how closely your actions will be aligned to your future destination. This will also increase the meaning you gain from your journey to that destination. A lot of people will only change when a particular situation occurs. If you want to transition to something new, you will need to make a logical and a psychological adjustment and that is more complex. As always though, it still requires you to take action.

At the end of the day, you are filled with a lot of content – information, ideas and experience. The nature of content is changing very rapidly and it is becoming obsolete so much more quickly. As individuals, we need to harness the skills from learning information rather than just acquiring more information.

Educators are finding that students who study a variety of subjects in school are having much more success after school because the different subjects teach different skill sets. For example, the processes you learn in science are very different to the creative skills you learn in art. Interestingly, some of the greatest scientists and artists have been very good at both science and art!

I could continue to give you compelling reasons to develop your sense of self, but ultimately, the responsibility rests with you and you deciding on whether or not you can believe in yourself. Once you develop a belief in yourself, you can then develop your ambition and this will determine how closely you will be aligned to your future direction and how you will gain meaning from your work.

However, if you don't believe in yourself, even just a little bit, you are unlikely to take any purposeful action. If you are feeling fear right now, I am taking you outside of your comfort zone. If you can believe in yourself, you will take the right risks.

At the end of the day, every suggestion or idea is worthless – unless you implement it! I am quite sure you have been in meetings where everybody has something to say, but you know full well that outcomes only occur when somebody does something!

Action 16: *Write down the names of at least two people who have believed in you. Write down what they believed about you and how that has inspired you on your journey so far. Consider contacting at least one person you know and telling them about your beliefs in their abilities*

_____

_____

_____

2.7 Sense Of Others

You may come from either an individualistic or a collectivist culture. In an individualistic environment, you are rewarded for your individual achievement. In a collectivist environment, you would feel a sense of achievement if the group around you achieves a result.

This is why some people from a collectivist culture shy away from the limelight and feel uncomfortable being one person representing multiple people. They find it difficult to explain how their efforts have led to the group's success. They would feel much happier if everyone in the group is given some form of recognition (or receives the reward).

In some very traditional collectivist cultures, one person will take all of their rewards and share it with the group before taking any for themselves. This is why generations of migrants have moved to other countries and yet still continue to send money home to look after the rest of their family.

Just because you have been brought up in an individualistic culture, it doesn't mean that you will want to keep every reward you receive for yourself. Some people still like to be the support person to someone else.

Some parents will work extra hard to provide significant opportunities for their children (although I would still encourage every parent to help children learn how to do things rather than simply provide things for them). Some families help each other buy a home or gain an education – others let each family member fend for themselves.

Understanding where you fit in your family and friends ecosystem is important. Every environment has positives and negatives. These environments also influence you in subconscious and conscious ways.

For example, you may have heard of the expression 'walking on egg-shells.' This is when someone has a feeling that what they do could easily upset someone else – so they adjust their behavior accordingly – because they have such a strong sense of the other person. Somewhere along the line, they find that they have lost their sense of themselves.

These people can often become trapped and even if they are given the chance to move away from a controlling environment, they find it difficult to be themselves because they haven't 'been themselves' before. If you are a person who is very sensitive to the needs of others, and you are in this situation, you may need some assistance to move forward in your own way – or you may simply need time to decide 'what is your way.'

To be able to attract the right career or business into your life, you will need to set up some boundaries. Boundaries are not something to fear. They are simply a framework to help you make decisions. If something appears within your boundary, you can say yes. If it is outside your boundary, you can say no. Your boundaries can also change as you learn and grow.

However, if you don't have any boundaries, you usually cannot say yes or no and you will have difficulty making decisions – either because you are not sure of yourself or what the people around you will think.

This will make it very difficult to attract the right career or business.

For example, I listened to the story of a woman who was in her early 50's and she had been running her own productivity based business for several years and ironically, she became burnt out. She was exhausted and overwhelmed because she had attracted too much work. So she found a person to prepare the business for sale and she sold it. Then she tried to go and find a 'normal job.'

Unfortunately, every time she got a job, she lost it. Every employer found her too competent so they terminated her employment. Then, she met a life coach. What she realized she needed was a better way to manage her own way of living and running a business, not find a 'normal job' instead.

So after a few months of coaching, she stopped looking for another job. She created more balance in her life (healthy eating, exercise, routines etc). Then she used her business acumen to start a new business more aligned to her new lifestyle and she is nearly 60. The best part is, she now feels like she is 50 again.

Action 17: *If you are going to attract the right career or business for your purpose, look at yourself in relation to the other people around you and how they are influencing your choices. If necessary, establish new boundaries so that you can make better decisions in the future*

3. Selecting The Right Career Or Business

The traditional view of career counselling or career development involves looking at you as an individual and utilizing various 'test and tell' tools to help you identify a future direction. I prefer to help you select a framework that you can use to calculate your own future direction.

I usually start by asking you to tell me about your story so far. I ask you a variety of questions and I write down some of the words from your answers. I ask you about your family of origin – what your parents and any siblings have done in their working life. I ask you to give me a history of what has happened so far in your working life and I listen very carefully for both challenging and rewarding events that have occurred along the way.

By listening without judgement, I gain a real sense of who you are as a person. I then ask a few questions to gain clarity around particular events and investigate in more detail some of the trials and tribulations as well as your major strengths.

I really like focusing on your strengths. I like differentiating between the strengths that you like to do as well as the strengths you have but don't like (for example, I am very good at accounting but I don't enjoy it).

If our discussion identifies some areas of weakness, I seek further clarification to see if these are real or perceived (for example, if you may have been in a very hostile environment for a long time, you may feel hopeless but you are not hopeless).

If there are weaknesses that could affect your future, we will briefly discuss how to overcome them, how to improve them or how to accept them and still move forward by focusing on your strengths. It is not a major element of our discussion but it is dealt with so that we can move on.

I also like to identify any items that you wish to include or not include in your future. One of my favorite interview questions when I was in recruitment was "What don't you want from this job?" For some people who find it difficult to think of what they do want, they usually find it very easy to describe what they don't want.

I really enjoy discussing the best aspects of your working life. The times when you felt congruent and in flow. These give me significant clues for even better questions to help you uncover your true values and purpose.

It is then time for either the two of us (or you on your own) to create a mind map. We start with a blank sheet of paper and we draw a circle in the middle and we write within the circle, your current non-negotiables.

If you are completely unsure about your non-negotiables (items you must have in your future), we simply start with a location of where you are wanting to work or do business. Otherwise, we might list a few variables – minimum annual income, major skill set to include, hours or lifestyle component etc.

We then record all of the other options you have ever thought about or completed in your life so far like branches from a tree in the middle. We record as many ideas as possible from your mind and put them on paper. We also record any particular things you want to avoid.

Did you know that 'words are the clothes of your thoughts?' By writing down all of these options, you are allowing your thoughts to be processed and for your subconscious mind to stop trying to sort and select them, especially when there is no framework or guidelines for sorting or selecting them.

Once the thoughts are out, it is time for you to relax and stop thinking about it at all. You do not need to do anything for a period of time. It could be 10 minutes, 10 hours, 10 days. Then you bring out the piece of paper again and with a different color pen or pencil, you can then circle the options that are most relevant to you right now. These elements give you the framework for your future decision making.

For example, when I did this exercise, my non-negotiables were:

- learning and teaching
- people and technology
- regular and passive income
- flexible hours and some travel
- future proof

My General Guidelines from all of the options from my past were:

- socially responsible
- newcomer related
- consulting
- training
- organizing events
- own website
- own books
- personal research

What I wanted to avoid included:

- autocratic environment
- rigid hours or location

What is most interesting about this exercise is that you can do it multiple times throughout your life. It is a way for you to understand yourself, to identify your skills and calculate your aligned options. Interestingly, in my case, it has remained current for a very long time – as you would expect because I have used a framework that honors my values and my purpose rather than an assessment that recommends some preferential choices based on my development up to that point.

Once you have become clear on the direction you would like to take, then we simply need to work out the steps involved.

Just remember that as you go through this process, you need to turn off the voices of the other people who live inside your head. You need to reflect on your past and what was real and what was perceived. You need to be kind to yourself and remember that you were doing the best you could at that moment in time. Try not to focus on past mistakes – just look at ways forward in the future.

It is a good idea to also do a bit of research to find out the current level of demand and supply and also the predictions for the future in your chosen direction (based on both qualitative and quantitative data, not anecdotes from your circle of friends).

You may not be 100% clear on what you want to do right now, so rather than wait until you are, you may start something as a bit of an experiment, particularly if you can do this on a part time or voluntary basis at first (I never recommend stopping everything you have done and trying to change completely overnight).

You can also look at the current market in an unbiased way and try and see if there are any stereotypes you may need to overcome. It may be technically too late to train to be a brain surgeon at 50, but some people may question why you want an entry level job in a different career at the same age. It is not impossible to achieve the second option, you just have to be aware that you may be up against society stereotypes and manage that risk accordingly.

A significant change will require you to persevere and it may be helpful if you enlist the support of a mentor or coach. Remember to personally thank everyone who gives you a referral or some assistance along the way and provide detailed feedback to referrers on a regular basis. Every so often, spend some time reviewing your progress to make sure that you are maintaining the right actions and strategies.

Action 18: *Either go through the Mind Map Process to define your future career or business or record it so that all of your future actions are in alignment with your future direction*

_____

_____

_____

4. Choosing What To Do Right Now

If you are currently in a career or business that is not congruent with your values, you can choose to either accept the situation, change the situation or leave and do something else. You have to work out how you can control the controllable and how you can adapt to the uncontrollable. You can also learn assertiveness skills or seek mediation if the situation is particularly bad.

When you are in an organization and you want to move your career along, you can aim to:

- move up with a promotion
- move sideways to increase your level of specialization
- realign yourself to an existing role
- move to another location

You could also leave or create a new opportunity and aim for something else.

However, before you make any changes, I encourage you to stop and think before you do anything. Firstly, if your current situation feels completely intolerable, you need to find just one simple small thing that is good about the job as a starting point.

For example, I was working with a young man who was in a contract project role with the Australian Army. He was not a trained soldier or officer and he was disappointed that the military was so regimented and formal in its approach. However, if he turns up to a job interview for a new job and is still bitter about his current job in the army, he is not going to be attractive to the new employer. They will sense his frustration, disappointment and need and he will be very unlikely to secure a new role.

What he loved about this role in the army was going out on 'jollies' on the army tanks, travelling across Australia and Asia and working with external stakeholders on complex projects. Once we dug a little deeper, what he was actually seeking was the next step up in his career and this is the value he brings to a new employer. If he makes this clear in his job interviews, that he is looking for a project management role that is more complex, more diverse and more collaborative, then he is immediately more attractive to the new employer. He is describing his value in terms that suit him and the employer, not providing negative details of what he wants to leave behind.

You also need to think about what you can do and what is best for you to do. I was helping a newly arrived migrant look for a senior executive role soon after he arrived in a new country. He had arrived on his own so that he could find work and then his wife and three children would join him later. Two of the children were almost teenagers and their youngest child was just a baby. I could have easily helped him find a senior executive role, but in all likelihood, that would have involved very long hours which would have had a very serious impact on his wife and family, especially as they were adjusting to life in a new country and English was not their first language.

So we agreed that the best thing for him to do was to find a slightly less demanding role so that he could secure work sooner and be an active part of his family's transition to the new country. Within just one year, he had a happy family and a new senior role aligned with his expertise. He chose to do what was best and sure enough, he attracted the right opportunity.

If we think about this at a more rational level, we can make an analogy with science and sales. This man had knowledge (science) but what he needed was techniques (sales) to achieve his goals. Likewise for you, don't just think about your skills, think about your value and how you can convey this value effectively.

To choose what to do right now, you may need to critically evaluate where you are at and stretch yourself a little further to achieve your goals. Ultimately, people will 'buy' something if experience, credentials or testimonials stack up. They will be able to detect whether or not you have the appropriate levels of authenticity, knowledge, skills, price, enthusiasm, energy and confidence. If they make a rash decision and buy anyway without this careful analysis and it turns out to be a mistake, you can rest assured they will not buy again. Smart purchasers know how to do all of these things first before buying.

Action 19: *Rather than choosing what to do at any point in time, start choosing what is best to do as a starting point. If you want to move to a new career or business, you need to showcase the value that is of most interest to the decision maker*

4.1 Choosing What To Do In The Future

Once you have clearly defined your values and your purpose from the previous sections, you will want to start planning what you will do in the future. You could start by writing down what you would consider doing in the next few months, within the next year and over the next 5-10 years.

I can tell you that when I left school, the only thing that I was clear about was that I wanted my career to involve some form of research. After spending the first 11 years working for the oldest bank in Australia and one of the 'big four,' I had a very rude awakening to the real world when I left the bank to move interstate. I was 28 and although I found a new job within six weeks, I was sacked shortly thereafter because I was pregnant. Then I couldn't find any work. To my complete surprise, as soon as my daughter was born, the phone started ringing with offers of employment.

I thought to myself at the time, this is completely ridiculous! I am in demand as a breast-feeding mother with a newborn baby and no family support and yet I could easily find myself on the scrap heap by the age of 40. That is when I vowed and declared I would keep learning new skills and keep myself up to date so that at any age in the future, I would be employable. I can assure you that I am now well past 40 and never out of work – and more importantly, never out of the type of work I want to do.

So let's go back to you. Where are you at right now? Do you have a Minimum Viable Product of information about you that is ready for the marketplace to view and consider? (In other words, are your details readily accessible to the people you would like to attract?) Furthermore, are you preparing your Best Viable Product resource that really sizzles 24 hours a day, seven days a week?

Are you aware of the opportunities that are available close by, a little further away, interstate or overseas, particularly if you would like to live, work or travel to a different location?

Are you building a professional reputation so that if someone else refers you to an aligned opportunity, the interested person can complete their own due diligence and verify your potential performance? Is it possible for the interested person to work out why they should consider you, why they should do it now and why they should make an offer to you? Have you included your contact information so that they can reach you directly?

Have you clearly defined your value and worked out ways to increase your value both now and in the future? Have you shown your value in a way that makes sense to the interested person? Have you showcased your results so that they can see what is possible?

If these questions have not been answered when the interested person is looking for your information, you won't 'make the sale.'

In the modern world, most of this information can be supplied online and I will explain how to do that in this book. Up until this point, you have possibly made some steps in the right direction and have been contemplating what might be worth doing next. Now is the time to carefully prepare the best steps to take in the future and then take action.

If you have not believed that you could take full ownership of this process, you may have learned how to be 'helpless.' You may have chosen to conserve your energy and reduce your risk and only take a few tentative steps here and there rather than take concrete action and risk being ridiculed. Don't worry. You can change right now.

I regularly tell people that the skills to find a job or business are very different to the skills to do a job or run a business. Helplessness does not equal hopelessness. If you can make good decisions and take action, you will move forward.

Making decisions can be difficult, especially if you do not feel secure about your future. I remember when I was about to leave my 19 year marriage (after extensive counselling and professional advice over many months) and I had to decide whether or not to sign a 12 month lease on a rental property. I did not have any intention of returning to the marriage (I would never do something so serious on a trial basis, especially as this was also going to affect my children), but in my mind, I only wanted a six month rental lease.

I contacted my second sister and asked for advice and she simply said, just make a decision and live with it. It sounded like such a simple task, but it terrified me. I guess I had been avoiding making a decision about the marriage for such a long time and now I really had to decide whether or not I was going to leave. I realized that every other choice

I had been making up to this point was part of this decision to leave so making this final decision was not such a big risk after all. I signed the lease and I stayed in that property for two years. It turned out to be the perfect location for my transition.

My sister's comment has been ringing in my head ever since. Just make a decision and live with it. How often have you avoided making a decision? Or do you make decisions without thinking of all of your options? Before I viewed this property for rent, I had already considered the best types of residence for my circumstances and this location was particularly suitable because it meant that the children could easily spend time with both their father and me and we have always shared their care equally. The best entrepreneurs in the world will often tell you that the main reason for their success is their ability to make decisions.

When thinking about your career or business, have you also looked at a range of options? Have you spoken to industry or profession experts? Have you sourced reputable labor market or business reports? Have you sought impartial advice from people who do not have a vested interest in a particular outcome? Personalizing your data collection for your unique circumstances will amplify your results. Relying on anecdotes is fraught with danger.

Ultimately, your ability to choose the right options for your future will be based on your natural and acquired capability, your level of enterprise and proactivity and your ability to clearly enunciate the value of what you have to contribute.

I am not suggesting that you should aim to be a superstar and seek a supernormal life. I am simply suggesting that if you collect the right information for the choices you want to make and then make a decision on what to do or not do next, then you have the best chance of completing the right steps to attract the right career or business.

Action 20: *Write down two of the worst decisions you have made in your life and why they were bad decisions. Then write down what you could have done at the time to make a better decision so that you can make better decisions in the future. Remember that one decision does not have the power to rule you for life*

_____

_____

5. Capital Raising

You may have heard that start-ups need to raise capital before they begin. Some start-ups begin without any capital at all! For you to attract the right career or business, you need to have a capital mindset – but I would like you to think beyond the concept of financial capital (money) and consider some of the other types of capital that are worth accumulating throughout your life.

Action 21: *Develop a capital raising mindset so that you can attract the right career and business opportunities*

5.1 Social Capital

My favorite is social capital. My definition of social capital is the good you share with other people. By creating this form of capital in your life, you will gain a sense of how you are a part of your community or tribe and you will develop a sense of belonging. I consider myself to be a social entrepreneur. Someone who applies business principles to social issues. I also believe that every person can benefit from completing voluntary work on a regular basis.

After working in a variety of voluntary roles over many years, I have noticed that many non-profit organizations waste a lot of time and energy and they often attract people with a particular agenda rather than a clearly defined outcome. I have also discovered that many volunteers in this environment are fearful of business practices because they associate business with profit rather than results.

Please do not let this put you off getting involved! In my view, a good social enterprise is sustainable and regularly delivers results, without relying on a few overworked individuals doing all of the work. So if you can contribute in some small way – even if it is only a few hours per month, the workload can be shared.

Many people have told me that the most meaningful work they have ever done has been completed voluntarily. Don't miss this wonderful opportunity to share your time and talents!

Action 22: *Choose the most relevant voluntary activities to complete on a regular basis so that you can develop a true sense of belonging and increase your social capital*

5.2 Intellectual Capital

There is one form of capital that you can never lose (unless a brain related illness occurs) and that is intellectual capital. You may lose all of your financial capital, but you can always start again with your intellectual capital. As I have discussed earlier in this book, your ability to constantly learn throughout your life will ensure that you remain available for opportunities as part of a career or business. Likewise, do not make the assumption that the only education worth securing is a formal education.

Whilst I am fortunate to have completed a Bachelor's Degree (by correspondence over seven years starting at the age of 26), I believe that my most valuable education has come from the hundreds of events that I have attended since completing my degree.

Studying in a formal sense is simply a process where you learn a skill or information and you are assessed for your ability to complete that skill or recall that information. In my view, applying what I have learnt in the real world is a much more complex task – so that is why I constantly learn more skills and information so that I can continue to apply them. I am a little selective nowadays and I focus on attending events or workshops that are related to my values and purpose.

I have also gone one step further to develop my intellectual capital – I teach. This gives me the incentive to stay one step ahead of my students and make sure that I am ready for their questions. By retaining my consulting practice, I can also provide real life examples in class and I tailor each course to the students in the room so that I can build on what they already know rather than overwhelm them with too much new information at once.

Action 23: *Choose the most relevant formal and informal education to complete in the future so that you can continue to develop your personal intellectual capital*

5.3 Cultural Capital

Cultural Capital is something that has developed in a unique way over time thanks to the fact that most of our communities have changed from being mono-cultural to multi-cultural, particularly in the last 200 years. An ability to understand other people and adapt to their personal style can be quite challenging if you have a fixed view of the world and associate certain actions and behaviors with clearly defined beliefs.

Culturally competent diverse societies have moved through the transitions of assimilation, tolerance and integration to inclusion. This has not been easy for everyone within these societies, especially people who have had to re-adjust under difficult circumstances or who have been happier living with a different model for a long time.

It is also important for me to include people who face personal cultural challenges due to their abilities (or disabilities), gender, sexual orientation, beliefs, native language or country of origin, socio-economic status or any other 'difference' to what is perceived as the norm for the society in which they live.

If you are able to develop a good level of cultural capital, you will be able to identify similarities rather than differences, you will be more willing to share than withhold and you will be exposed to a greater range of possibilities and opportunities because you will be able to gain insights beyond your standard frame of reference.

Cultural capital could be the hardest capital for you to acquire, particularly if you have had negative experiences in the past. I am pleased to be able to say that my level of cultural capital has allowed me to enjoy the most amazing experiences – because they are so unique and unexpected. That said, I have also been able to recognize and respect my origins and see the value in that culture as well – as an Australian, I am so grateful that I live in a civilized country and I truly believe that our culture is well worth sharing!

Action 24: *Find out how you can increase your cultural capital (or cultural exposure) so that you can receive greater insights and opportunities beyond your standard frame of reference*

5.4 Financial Capital

Financial Capital is often showcased as the main capital of success. It can include actual money as well as assets that generate income. Another way to think of money is 'crystallized time.' The way I see it, financial capital is a combination of both time and money. Some people have more time and less money, others have more money and less time. Either way, financial capital is a form of exchange in most western societies.

A certain level of financial capital is required to simply survive in modern society. In civil societies, there is a reasonably good safety net for people who find themselves without financial capital for a period of time. In other societies, a safety net does not exist. Sometimes a safety net exists but the person in crisis chooses not to use it.

It has been said before that the quality of a society can be measured by the way it treats the people who are poor in that society. Like many other people, I believe that education is the main way to help someone move forward.

However, I have been in the situation where my immediate need was to survive. At that point, any form of education would have been completely useless. You cannot imagine how grateful I was to be politely and sensitively invited to go to a food bank and be encouraged to collect a variety of grocery items free of charge. What was even better was that both the essential items I needed (fruit, vegetables, bread and milk) were available, but also some items that I considered to be extremely exotic (and never on my shopping list because they were beyond my budget). They even had pre-prepared meals available so on some occasions, I didn't even have to cook (what a luxury!).

Through the food bank, I had my very first taste of goat's cheese. It was divine. That tiny treat gave me the first glimpse that I would be able to move past this dark phase in my life. As soon as I was able to manage again on my own, I stopped going to the food bank. I do not believe in encouraging people to live on perpetual hand-outs, but I sincerely believe that a hand-up at the right time can make all the difference. It can be a catalyst for change and provide a pathway to growth.

Have you also noticed that some people, no matter how much money comes into their life, their financial position never changes? I would like to suggest that if you are one of these people, you may need to learn how to delay gratification. You may have become accustomed to spending money rather than saving money. My father once told me that you don't save money by spending money (I was a teenager being seduced by some very clever discount advertising at the time).

If you would like to start this process, begin with small savings. One of the best pieces of advice I have ever received is don't buy anything until you absolutely need it. By delaying all of my purchases for as long as possible (including regular groceries), I have found ways to make do with what I already have, go without, to borrow something instead, to rent rather than buy, to work on an exchange basis or come up with a different solution entirely. Even if I have to eventually purchase an item at a higher price than what I could have when I first had the need, because I have managed to avoid so many expenses, I have still been much better off financially and I have saved a fortune (and lived more simply with a lot less clutter).

I can also tell you for a fact that I have survived on an average taxable income of just AUD26,000 per year for five years from 2005 to 2010 when more than 50% of my income was used to pay the rent. I was also supporting myself and two children, did not have access to childcare and I started with a debt of $20,000 (which I also paid off during this time). I even went on a few short vacations.

When one of my clients wondered whether or not she should start a family or continue working full time after recently arriving in Australia (her husband was a highly paid expatriate working for an international consulting firm), I politely suggested she would be able to manage, because there are plenty of low cost options for raising children but once you get past a certain age, having children becomes difficult. To my delight, not only did she secure suitable work that matched her new lifestyle immediately, she made time to create a fantastic social network to support both her and her husband in their new country and she became pregnant almost instantly!

What I am essentially suggesting here is that if you want to attract the right career or business and you currently feel that financial capital is stopping you, consider re-assessing how you spend your existing income, how you can live more simply and how you can adjust your lifestyle so that you can live according to your true values.

Financial planners and advisers will tell you about the people they have met who have plenty of money and are living a life full of regret because of all of the things they wished they had done rather than pursue financial security. A bad investment or business decision can easily destroy your financial capital in an instant. A life full of meaning and purpose can never be taken away. Remember that some of the happiest people on this earth have the least money (however, please be realistic and make sure that you can still survive without undue stress on you and your loved ones).

You may have heard the story about the Greek fisherman who was happy spending part of his week fishing for his small business and the rest of his time enjoying his life with his family and friends. A savvy businessperson suggested that he could improve his small business, have a fleet of boats and earn a fortune and the fisherman said why? The businessperson said, 'so you can relax and have more time with your family and friends.' The irony was, he had that already – he didn't need the savvy businessperson's advice at all!

Action 25: *Have a realistic look at how you have managed your financial capital in the past and decide whether or not you need to make any changes so that you will be in a position to attract the right career or business that is aligned with your true values in the future*

5.5 Gratitude Or Operating Capital

There is a great deal of pop psychology encouraging us to be grateful for everything that we have. Previous generations have lived through horrendous atrocities, wars, famines, diseases and challenges and after these crises, they have learnt what is most important in life. What really is important and how to be grateful for your current lifestyle.

Gratitude (or Operating) Capital is something that many people forget to acknowledge and record. It is often a type of capital that people only recognize when it is taken away. For example, you may not realize how fortunate you are to be able to walk, but if you ever lose the ability to walk, you will realize that you should have been grateful for that ability in the past.

In the darkest phase of my life, I could not see any goodness around me at all. I could not see any way out of my circumstances, despite all of the things I had done to overcome my challenges. I came to the conclusion that there was no point trying to continually fight this war any more. I had to look at what I did have rather than what I didn't have. I chose to change my outlook on life and I started by trying to identify as many gestures of kindness as possible.

What I thought would 'rescue' me from my dire situation was financial capital. As it turns out, gratitude capital got me out of my mess. Here are just some of the gestures of kindness I observed:

- A friendly smile for no reason from complete strangers
- Interesting casual conversations on public transport
- Unexpected courtesies, like allowing me to jump the shopping queue because I only had one item to purchase or regularly being let in during heavy traffic
- Helpful suggestions and friendly chit chat rather than annoying sales pitches when I was out and about
- Generosity when sharing information or answering questions at free events
- Personal offers of help (which I had previously ignored)
- A surprise gift from a client with a hand written card, personally delivered on the weekend
- Regular phone calls from friends
- Invitations to dinner, lunch or coffee and I wasn't allowed to pay

When I started recognizing and acknowledging these gestures, I found even more things to be grateful for in my life. I am healthy and have all of my faculties. I have two healthy children. I have food to eat and a roof over my head. I live in one of the best and safest countries in the world. I have wonderful friends and an extended family that is also living according to their values. I have meaningful work to do every day (paid and unpaid).

When I looked around me, I could see that other people were grateful for other things. There is no right or wrong way to assess the value of your gratefulness. An older friend who had lived through the Great Depression was grateful for every single meal he ate because he knew what it was like to be really hungry and be uncertain about when he would eat again.

You may already know that people who regularly write down what they are grateful for are significantly more positive about their future than people who don't write it down. Whilst I don't always write down what I am grateful for now, whenever I have some time to contemplate my life, I look around and identify all of the wonderful things around me at that moment. I feel truly blessed.

Action 26: *Write down three things you are most grateful for in your life right now. Consider how these three things have led to your current level of success and enable you to keep going or can help you attract the right career or business in the future*

_____

_____

_____

5.6 Relationship Capital

Have you ever stopped to think about how important it is to have the people you know in your life? Your best friends, family members and peers? The encouragement and the challenges that they share make your life interesting and meaningful.

The relationship I have with my children is the most important of my life. At different times in our lives, other people are a priority – especially when they have a crisis and need our support.

For parents of children, I sometimes suggest that your partner is the most important person in your life, but when your children are young, the children are your priority. It is up to you to decide which people in your life are important and which ones have priority.

It is also important to realize the value, both positive and negative of some of these people. If their negative behavior encourages you to grow, it can be worthwhile. If it is destroying you personally, it will make it extremely difficult to attract the right career or business.

Building capital in this area takes a certain amount of commitment and strength. If you are not in a relationship now and you know that a new relationship would be nice, are you creating opportunities for that to happen? Do you need a coach, advisor or mentor? Do you need an accountability partner? Do you need to reduce the amount of time you spend with someone who is having a negative influence on your life?

Sometimes it is difficult to stop spending time with some of the people in our relationships circle. You may be working with someone and there is no way to avoid them apart from leaving your job. You may have a close family member living with you and you may need to accept them as they are but reduce their level of influence over you. There may be a friend that you keep because of the good parts even when you know that their bad parts are worse and these are affecting you but you stay connected because of a fierce sense of loyalty.

I cannot suggest which relationships you need to keep and which relationships you need to change or cease. After spending time with victims of domestic violence, I can tell you that it can be extremely difficult to change your life and it usually takes a lot of help and time and as irrational as it may seem to others, many victims choose to stay in these difficult relationships. They have often become accustomed to the status quo and they tell themselves that deep down, the abuser loves them.

As I have said previously, the more you value yourself, the more value you will attract. There are many support services around to help you learn good relationship skills, parenting skills and management skills. Don't be afraid to treat relationship capital as a key target area to increase on your mission to attracting the right career or business. Collect the knowledge and wisdom you need to make this a strong feature of your life. By increasing your relationship capital, you will also increase the relationship capital of the people around you.

Action 27: *Reflect on the most important people in your life right now and the people who are your highest priority. Are they helping or hindering your progression? Write down three things you could to improve your relationship capital*

_____

_____

_____

5.7 Credibility Capital

Do you have a position of significance amongst your friends, family and peers? How did you gain this credibility? What encouraged these people to identify your skill or capability as genuine? Have you ever been in a position where your credibility was questioned?

Trust is a currency. Loyalty is an asset. Credibility generates returns. If people believe that you are credible, you will be able to attract the right career or business. They will believe what you or your business tells them.

For most people, credibility is established after multiple repeated behaviors. If you continually arrive on time, it is probably safe to assume that you are likely to arrive on time again and if you don't arrive on time, then something is unusual. If you consistently perform well in your role, I am likely to recommend you for another similar role.

Credibility is an historical concept. It is based on what you have done. If you repeatedly perform at your best, even if it is not perfect, most people will believe you are credible. They will be accepting of minor flaws. If you constantly promise and never deliver, you will have no credibility. If you say something and never take responsibility for carrying through, you will have no credibility.

I have a very dear friend that I appreciate enormously. However, he often says he will do something and then he never does it, even when I remind him about his promise. He tells me that he didn't promise, he only said something. Unfortunately, whenever he tells me he will do something now or in the future, I will not believe it.

I have also had my credibility challenged. I have had complaints lodged against me based on perceptions not facts. To face the accusers, I had to provide evidence that contradicted their perceptions. Fortunately, I was able to do this and I have maintained my credibility.

I believe credibility is also related to honesty, ethics and professionalism. We should all aspire to being honest at all times. We should all aspire to the highest standards of ethics and not be guided by self-interest. We should all act professionally, even when we are in a highly charged emotional state or at risk of suffering financially.

Credibility can be maintained if you follow these principles. If you lose your credibility, I believe it takes twice as long to regain it – before people will trust you again and believe what you say and do. I encourage you to act responsibly at all times to maintain your credibility – it will help you attract the right career or business.

Action 28: *Reflect on the people and businesses you know that you believe are highly credible. What do these people do and say that helps you believe that they are credible? What could you do to be more credible?*

_____

_____

_____

5.8 Influence Capital

Over time, everyone develops a range of skills. Some people choose to specialize in a certain area, other people like to develop a range of skills or move into a managerial or leadership role. Most people reach a stage in life where they would like to be significant in some way and leave a legacy.

A legacy does not need to be a grand monument to significant achievement. Every day, we have the opportunity to influence the people around us. We can wake up with a smile or a frown. We can be pleasant or cranky. We can believe that we are a victim of our circumstances or we can choose what to do next regardless of our circumstances.

Leadership is a choice, not a title or an entitlement. We can choose to lead by example – preferably a positive example. As children, we naturally observed and mimicked the behavior around us and it is a natural instinct for us to keep doing this throughout our lives.

Think carefully. What bad behaviors do you still pick up from others? What bad behaviors do you demonstrate to others?

If you are willing to raise your level of influence capital, you will be willing to make conscious choices about what you do and say. You will understand that everything you do has an influence on you and the people around you. You will understand that the more you raise your standards, so too you will raise the standards around you. Then, you will notice that the right career and business opportunities will suddenly start to find you.

Action 29: *By increasing the standards of your own behavior, you will influence your own outcomes and the effect your behavior has on the people around you. Increasing your influence capital will increase the number of career and business opportunities that appear in your life*

6. Action Steps

Selecting the relevant steps for the next part of your career or business attraction journey will hopefully fill you with anticipation and excitement! Now that you have a better understanding of your own background, future direction and the capital resources available, I would like to help you with the actual action steps. Remember, I can make helpful suggestions, but is up to you to accept responsibility and take action towards achieving your goals!

Action 30: *Suggestions will only be helpful to you if you accept responsibility for completing the associated actions*

6.1 Research And Select Your Locations

Now that you are clearer about your future direction, you need to find out a bit more information about your preferred options and also your contingency 'Plan B' options. As you go through this research phase, seek unbiased quantitative and qualitative information from a variety of sources to help you refine your plans accordingly.

For example, I was working with a man in his late 40's who had originally started his career as a scientist. However, one of his very first supervisors identified that he had excellent sales skills and encouraged him to consider a change of career. Despite a range of company takeovers, mergers and acquisitions, he successfully secured consecutive sales roles across Australia for the next 25 years in one particular industry.

However, he had reached a roadblock and although he was still securing interviews, he was not able to secure his next full time role. He had an intimate knowledge of this industry and he had seen it steadily decline and the number of sales opportunities dry up. So we had to source a new solution.

We discovered that his chance to secure a similar role would be difficult as so many enterprises in his industry had been swallowed up by conglomerates and the sales process was changing dramatically. We also discovered that there was a very real opportunity to shift his skills into selling his value proposition rather than a company's products.

We quickly identified that there would be a variety of enterprises that could call on his expertise in a consulting role (for example, accountancy and legal practices specializing in mergers and acquisitions where the 'new' organization had to also readjust the sales process) and as it turns out, he was particularly interested in shifting from a full time sales role to a consulting practice as he also had an extensive network and long standing business relationships and was starting to think about retirement.

As he was able to identify multiple transferable skills, he could also apply these skills to other industry groups. As soon as he started contacting people, everything fell into place. If he had stuck to his original idea of finding a sales role in the same industry, he may have been 'stuck' for a lot longer.

This research is essential pre-work or homework you need to do before the next step. You may also find that you need to complete further study (especially if you need to secure a higher level of accreditation or professional association membership) and you need to start collecting all of your documentation. This could include:

- Academic transcripts and certificates from your courses and qualifications
- LinkedIn recommendations or written references
- Comprehensive details of your previous experience including dates, organization names and descriptions, job titles, tasks, achievements and website addresses
- The login details for all of your online records (social media profiles, job seeking websites, blogs, websites, online directories etc)
- Professional association membership details (start date, level of membership, membership number etc)
- A comprehensive list of your past publications

A good pro forma for compiling this information is to look at all of the information that you can add to a LinkedIn Profile http://linkedin.com. I believe that everyone should consider having a LinkedIn Profile. I was one of the first 80,000 people in the world to join LinkedIn in 2003 and I have found it extremely useful for my own career and business and I have helped hundreds of other people secure amazing opportunities through the platform.

Depending on the nature of the career or business you are seeking, now is the time to work out which online and offline platforms that are likely to be most helpful to you. Where you know the decision makers can be found and where they will be looking for you.

My personal view is that everyone should consider having their own name website or blog. I have created my own website at http://sueellson.com (and I pay a fee to host this website). If you want to get started with a free option, I recommend that you create a free website or blog at http://wordpress.com – this can easily be exported to your own name website in the future.

If you are not quite ready yet, I still encourage you to register your own name domain name (called an 'exact match domain name') if it is available. My personal preference is for a .com domain name but this is not always available.

This initial phase of collecting and publishing all of this information may seem tedious, but I can assure you that most of my clients who take the time to go through this process find it very rewarding. It is a fantastic way to consolidate your thoughts and make sense of your journey so far. It helps you remember what has worked well in the past and it is a great way to reflect on your achievements.

Once you have gone through this process, maintaining your records will be much easier because you will have a framework for sorting and collating the information as it occurs in the future. It may take time to reconstruct your story. There may even be pieces that you have forgotten. For now, focus on the essential details and compile and collect the specific details over time.

Action 31: *Complete the necessary qualitative and quantitative research associated with your chosen career or business, assess this detail, select the places where you will share this information and then collect the information you need to add to the various online and offline platforms*

6.2 Establish Quality Real Estate

We all understand that life is always much nicer if you can live in a nice place. Even if you have a very ordinary house, unit or apartment, you can still make it presentable and comfortable by ensuring that it is clean and tidy and well kept.

If you want to attract decision makers to your online and offline profiles, you need to make sure that they are relevant and well kept.

Everyone has an offline profile. It comes in the form of relationships, memberships and regular appearances at various locations (work, study, interest groups, leisure activities etc). By turning up in everyday life, you have an opportunity to be noticed and invited to consider a career or business opportunity. I will discuss more of these in detail in Section 12.

What can be extremely helpful in the attraction phase of a career or business is your online profile. Now more than ever, people are capturing opportunities for life, love, work and soul online. It is the main conduit between the economies I discussed in Section 2.1 – the Gig, Attention, Reputation, Referral, Sharing, Knowledge, Demand and Social Economies. If you can exist outside of these economies, you can skip an online profile – if you want to maximize them, you need an online profile, as soon as possible.

There are certain guidelines you should follow when creating and maintaining your profiles. I encourage you to:

- choose and complete profiles that are relevant to your purpose and the decision makers you wish to attract
- use good quality photos, logos, images etc that have been optimized to load quickly and are the best size and style for the screen space on a desktop or mobile device
- provide accurate, relevant and consistent content (more about this in Section 10)
- maintain it on a reasonably regular basis – aim for quality and relevance rather than quantity and frequency
- focus on what you can keep that will be archived indefinitely (your own website) and reaching out to where your decision making audience could be looking for you (other websites and platforms)
- set realistic goals that you can achieve – there is no point over-extending yourself in the beginning and then having out of date content after you have secured the first opportunity
- be willing to adapt to the changing nature of the online world – search and platform algorithms are constantly

changing so you need to be abreast of the most significant changes that affect your attraction methods – avoid seeking vanity results

- be prepared to experiment, test, assess and review your methodology over time – new options will appear and if you want to be at the 'front of the pack,' you need to be willing to be a relatively early adopter

- think very carefully before joining a paid platform (or even a free platform) because all platforms require some level of involvement from you (even if you outsource some components). Time and experience is still a cost – always ask yourself, is this relevant (and reliable) for my purpose?

Action 32: *Based on your very clear purpose and the most effective online and offline platforms for attracting the right decision makers for your career or business, complete your selected profiles in an accurate, reliable and consistent format*

6.3 Review And Verify Your Real Estate

As you go through the process of completing your online and offline profiles, you will gather a range of new ideas worth considering. You will find that some profiles offer an extensive array of sections to complete and they may also offer profiles within a profile (e.g. LinkedIn allows you to have a Person and a Company Profile and set up a Group). This is why it is a good idea for you to select and complete all of your profiles and then go back over each of them and improve them with the ideas you have collected from the other profiles.

For example, you will find that you need to provide various size images (so create these as you go and have them handy for any future profiles). You will need short, long and medium length descriptions (and these should be consistent across the platforms and include the primary and secondary keywords you would like to optimize in each profile). You will find that some profiles require very specific information (like your Certification or Registration Number) and by adding this information to your other profiles, you are signaling to the decision maker that all the information they need is right here, right now.

It is also important for you to ask other people – friends, colleagues and professionals to give you feedback on your profiles. There may be subtle changes that you can make that will greatly increase your likelihood of appearing in search results or being contacted for opportunities (you need to find the most important sections for search words and you must include your contact details and a call to action in a publicly accessible location on every profile).

When you receive this feedback, keep a written record and then reflect on whether or not their suggestions match your research findings and your purpose (remember that their feedback is likely to have a component of personal preference). Ultimately it is up to you to decide how you want to be viewed by decision makers.

For example, I was working with a woman who runs a rehabilitation clinic for people who wish to overcome drug or alcohol addictions. Google search methodology encourages advisers like me to optimize her clinic for the location where it is based. However, her clients come from all over the city, not just that particular suburb. So although my advice to her was to optimize her content for her suburb, she needed to optimize her content for the city. Whilst your friend may know the keywords for their industry, they don't necessarily know the key trigger points in your industry. Cultural norms for content in the USA are very different to cultural norms in different European countries.

Action 33: *After completing your online and offline profiles, revisit each profile and add in more details and then ask a variety of people to review your details so that you can tweak it even further based on your research and purpose*

6.4 Select Your Strategic Activity

Every profile you create will give you different opportunities. Some will simply allow you to provide current information (that you need to keep current by reviewing it at least once a year). Other profiles will allow you to participate – to like, comment, share, post, publish, rate, review, recommend, refer, endorse, network etc. You need to think about the types of activity that will fulfil your purpose.

For example, by adding a post, you may have 'life time' value but if you 'share' content it may only have 'real time' dynamic value. However, the platform algorithms may give preference to your profile if you regularly share content but only give you limited exposure from your involvement in a group or your 'lifetime' post. If your desire is to connect with an individual who has a very strong identity in a group and very little involvement with looking at an individual profile, you may never reach that person by writing a post.

The safest option is to choose a range of relevant concurrent strategies that serve both a static and a dynamic purpose. Static purposes can usually be achieved by providing quality content, information or resources at least three times a year. Dynamic purposes should be calculated so that you can get the maximum return on your investment. For example, clicking 'like' will give you very little dynamic value. If you review the item, like, comment and share it, you are much more likely to be rewarded by the algorithms.

Understanding the nuances of each platform is an area of expertise in itself. Naturally, my desire is for you to spend most of your time doing what you love not learning how to attract what you love. However, most people in any form of enterprise will tell you that up to 80% of their time is spent on attracting the right opportunities from the right target audience.

If you are able to master the most relevant attraction strategies for your purpose, it is my belief that you can reduce this to a maximum of 20% of your time. This figure includes the amount of time you need to keep learning and growing to maintain your level of targeted attraction.

I have seen a lot of capable people try and learn all of these techniques by going to various courses, workshops and seminars and sitting through hours of irrelevant information that in the end, confuses them and they eventually get stuck in analysis paralysis.

In my view, you will save yourself a lot more time and energy if you are clear on your purpose and then you source one-on-one personal support from a professional who specializes in your target platform.

When you meet with this person (in person or virtually), you can clearly describe your requirements and then they can show you the most important techniques for achieving your purpose. It may cost you more upfront in terms of dollars spent, but you will save yourself hours of time and energy and you will secure better results sooner.

For example, I had a woman who was attending a course I ran on Creating a Simple WordPress Website. She was a journalist and had spent her entire career writing for mainstream publications. She was confused by WordPress and felt that she needed to learn what it was about so that she could transition from writing for a publication to writing for herself. After attending the two day course, she realized she was not a website designer – but she did gain enough knowledge to give a website designer an accurate briefing for the design, layout and search engine optimization strategy for her new website.

She carefully selected a suitable professional to build her website and she was up and running almost instantly (and very happy with the outcome as I met her on a follow up course I ran on Promoting Your Website Free of Charge). She is a perfect example of collecting enough knowledge to be able to secure the right services from an appropriately qualified professional. She gained enough knowledge to make sure that she did not overpay and she received a quality product on time and on budget with all of the necessary strategic functions built in. She took ownership of her project, she acquired the knowledge she needed to continue her purpose and then once the first step was completed, she moved forward with the next step of attracting more decision makers to her content.

Action 34: *Select a range of life time and real time activities that you can complete (or outsource) on a manageable and regular basis so that you can maximize your attraction power. Gaining preliminary ownership level knowledge and then hiring a professional on an individual basis will be quicker and more effective than trying to do everything yourself*

6.5 Review, Analyze and Improve

Once you have gone through the first four stages and you have been using your various strategies for at least three months, you will find that certain techniques deliver better results than others.

Some techniques will not be measurable at all and that is not a reason to eliminate them. Remember the philosophy that if you can't tie knots, tie lots. Sometimes opportunities occur simply because you have taken several actions rather than because you have taken a specific action. Every reaction is not necessarily attributable to one particular action. You may like to test and try a few different options at different times on different platforms.

However, if you have noticed that some platforms are working much more effectively for you than others, you may like to review an individual platform, analyze its performance and consider ways to improve the performance even further. This may even involve paying for additional services from the platform. After all, if a payment generates an even better return, why wouldn't you consider paying for more of the right opportunities to come your way – especially if they help you achieve your highest values?

A classic example of this is Facebook advertising. Another one of my website course participants had a tourism related business and she found that Facebook was able to help her reach her exact target audience at distinct moments in time. She created a tailor-made paid advertisement targeting well organized women in the local area inviting them to purchase a special Mother's Day Limited Time Offer several weeks before Mother's Day. She then created a different advertisement targeting disorganized men in the local area inviting them to purchase a special Mother's Day Last Minute Offer just days before Mother's Day. She sold lots of tickets on both occasions.

This businesswoman freely admitted that she only guessed that this would work – she didn't base her decision on hard data, just her past experience and knowledge of ticket buying trends leading up to Mother's Day. However, as a result of having direct access to a very specific target audience, she attracted the exact type of business she wanted from the exact type of audience willing to pay. She had to 'pay to play' but she still earned a profit. I should also add that she had the ability to craft an excellent quality Facebook advertisement (with a great image with overlaid text) and she knew enough about Facebook advertising from her past experience to carefully select the relevant target demographic and display it at the right time.

Action 35: *After using various platforms for at least three months, review and analyze the performance and results. Find ways to improve your efficiency and effectiveness. Also consider 'pay to play' options*

6.6 Give Feedback, Follow Up, Say Thank You And Smile

I have already talked about Gratitude Capital and the importance or reflecting on what you are grateful for in life.

If you are willing to give positive and descriptive feedback, I can assure you that you will be remembered. It will open the doorway to even more attraction.

I also believe that 20% of your attraction strategy should involve following up with the people you have already attracted! Everybody knows that the best source of new business or opportunity is from your existing network or clients, especially if they have been happy with your past offerings! You have already spent time and effort attracting these people, so make sure you maintain that relationship.

There are many ways you can follow up. You can contact people directly – in person, by phone, SMS, email, a printed card sent in the post or a direct message in their favorite online platform. You can automate the process by sharing quality content in an automatic fashion – regular news updates, posts, newsletters or new connections. You can send a virtual or real gift – an endorsement, a recommendation, rating, review, physical goods (flowers, chocolates, a hamper) or a special experience ticket (movie, theatre, activity) provided it is not seen as a bribe and complies with local governance requirements.

One of the most important parts of any follow up is to say thank you. If you want to reinforce good behavior, you need to recognize and reward good behavior. I encourage you to go out of your way to say thank you on a regular basis, wherever you go and regardless of what you are doing. Once you get into the habit, your life will change – for the better! Be on the lookout all the time so that you can personally acknowledge every other person's contribution.

Be willing to recognize a job well done – even if it was completed by a competitor! Remember, there is enough for everyone. The birds in the trees don't go out to work each day to pay for groceries at the store – but they do wake up every day and manage to find the food and drink that each one of them needs to survive.

People who like to think a lot often forget to smile. I remember watching a YouTube video that was sent to me by one of my clients and she asked me to provide some feedback. What the guy said in the video was actually very interesting, but he said all of it without a smile. If I hadn't been asked to provide feedback, I would never have finished watching that video.

Have you ever noticed that successful people always seem to be smiling? How it looks as if they have just returned from a fabulous holiday on a remote beach on a private island? Have you ever noticed how attractive people are when they smile? Can you hear a smile (or a frown) in someone's voice on the radio, phone or in a podcast?

The best part about smiling (and its cousin, laughter), is that it makes you feel better! Even if you don't feel like smiling, smile anyway. Remember that your brain can't tell the difference between what is real and what is imagined. I can guarantee that you will be instantly more attractive if you smile.

Make a point of making sure that the first time a person sees you, you are smiling. Think back to the best leaders you have spent time with – did they smile at you? Did they give you descriptive feedback? Did they follow up? Did they say thank you for your contribution?

Action 36: *Find ways every day to give descriptive feedback, follow up with people you already know, say thank you and smile. It will change your life for the better!*

6.7 Celebrate, Acknowledge And Learn

If you have been in 'survival' mode for any length of time, it is highly likely that you have stopped celebrating any of your victories. You may have got to a point where you don't think that there is anything worth celebrating, not even your birthday (yes, you are another year older – but you are also wiser and you are still alive).

A lot of people fall into the trap of thinking that the only time they can celebrate is when they have achieved a significant milestone. I completely disagree. Some of the greatest moments in my life were simply a short moment in time.

For example, I remember sending off my last university assignment for my last university subject. It was a research project that ultimately led to the development of my first website Newcomers Network http://newcomersnetwork.com and I had put my heart and soul into the final document. This project was giving me the platform for my future enterprise and I was so excited about what would happen in the future. I received a High Distinction.

As it turns out, my entire degree was completed by correspondence, so apart from attending a one day Orientation Session at the University before I started, I did not complete any of my degree on campus. After completing my degree, I was invited to attend a Graduation Ceremony and to be perfectly honest, I didn't feel the need to attend at all. As far as I was concerned, I had already achieved the result I was seeking and I had celebrated in my own way.

However, my parents really wanted me to attend. So, I travelled interstate, hired a gown and received my university degree certificate in front of a large audience that included two grandparents, my parents and my ex-husband. I still did not feel that this celebration was necessary.

What I can tell you is that after the ceremony, I can distinctly remember how proud my parents and grandparents were that I had completed a degree. As it turns out, I was the first of 27 grandchildren to receive a degree and I was 35 years old at the time. After the ceremony, a slightly larger group (including my brother, his wife and some friends) joined us for dinner and we all had a fabulous time. So even though I did not feel like celebrating, the opportunity to join in the entire celebration process meant that several other people also had an enjoyable opportunity – including me!

I can now look back on this experience and realize the value of celebrating. I also look for ways to acknowledge effort, even if a desired outcome does not occur. When you are in your own business, I can assure you that you will probably try a lot of things and many of them will not work! That is not a reason to ignore the effort you made – it is simply important to acknowledge what does and doesn't work and learn from the experience rather than repeat the wrong thing over and over again.

I believe you also need to acknowledge your personal wins. The times when you step outside of your comfort zone, feel the fear and do it anyway. It sometimes takes bravery and courage to complete a task. I also believe that the bravest people in the world are not the people who do the most significant things. I believe that the bravest people in the world are those that tackle what they fear the most.

To me, the task could be quite simple, but for them, it could seem incredibly frightening. When I see these people complete that scary task, I watch them transform. The first task doesn't always lead to an outcome, but the increase in clarity and confidence that they gain is huge! Progress has occurred. On some occasions, I have become so excited, it has brought me to tears. Even as I write this, I feel like the proud mother who has just watched my son or daughter achieve a milestone. If you know someone who has faced a fear and still taken action, remember to acknowledge their effort and celebrate it, regardless of how insignificant it may appear to others.

Action 37: *Remember to celebrate victories, acknowledge achievements and learn what does and doesn't work. Do this for yourself and for others*

6.8 Decide What To Do Next

After you have been through the action step cycle for the first time, you need to look at everything you have learnt and enjoy the celebrations, but you then need to make some decisions around what you are going to do next.

The cycle of life is repeated frequently and if you are aware and conscious, each time the cycle repeats, you will have an opportunity to grow and develop a little more and make use of what you have learnt in more productive ways.

If you don't make some new choices, you risk facing similar challenges and you also risk losing some opportunities. You may think, how could I lose opportunities? I did it once, surely I can just repeat it and do it again?

Unfortunately, no. The reality is that life is constantly changing. Yes, there are some seasons that come and go and cycles that repeat fairly consistently, but on any given day, the weather can change. Our environment is being affected by our personal choices (I won't start the global warming debate here).

Consciously, I also believe humans are changing and growing – so each time we reach the next level, we need to decide how we are going to move forward.

So each time your action cycle reaches this point, pause and take a moment to reflect and consider the new choices you will make in the future. It is an empowering and enlightening feeling. You can look back and see how you have improved and what new skills you have developed. You can see what you have gained and what you have lost. Most importantly, you can start again – with more wisdom. Your challenges have improved you. Your moments of bliss have inspired you. The future is coming.

Action 38: *After completing each action step cycle, pause and make some decisions on what you will do next so that you can continue to attract the right career or business opportunities*

7. Career Attraction Tips and Techniques

If you would like to attract the right career, you need to attract decision makers who are seeking your skills, knowledge, networks and attitude. You need to be appealing to 'head hunters' – either professional head hunters working for a recruitment agency or decision makers (business owners or human resource professionals) looking for someone with the value you offer.

The most successful recruitment strategy, for many years, has been to ask existing employees to recommend someone they know for a current or upcoming vacancy. This is an extremely effective technique because the existing employee already understands the enterprise culture, expectations and requirements. This strategy also delivers the best retention results.

One of the most important elements of a personal employee referral strategy is recommending someone with the right attitude. Most people can be taught a new skill. Adjusting a person's attitude is much more difficult. Good recruitment leads to good retention. That is why savvy decision makers spend more time selecting the right person and less time sacking and replacing the wrong person.

As a recruiter, I was taught that past performance is the best predictor of future behavior. When I have been in a recruitment role, I have spent most of my time looking for candidates that have transferable skills, relevant achievements and a congruent work ethic. I like to understand the candidate's level of perseverance, flexibility, adaptability and willingness to be proactive. I look for indicators of their ability to cooperate, to lead or follow, to be committed and to be loyal for the duration of the role.

I also like to assess whether or not they will fit in to their new environment and if they are ready for this transition. This does not mean that they have to be identical to the other employees in the enterprise. It simply means that they have to be able to demonstrate how they can share their value effectively and respectfully. I will be making my decision based on a reasonable level of risk.

For example, they could be wild, creative and dogmatic or they could be unique, challenging and friendly. Either one of these individuals could be a suitable match for an organization, but as the recruiter, I need to know which one would bring the best value to the organization seeking the new employee.

If you would like to attract the right career, you need to be very clear about the type of people you would like to work with and the type of enterprise you would like to join. You need to have moved past any old issues and regrets. If you have, you can then tailor your strategy and attract the right employers and eliminate enquiries from the wrong employers. If you can clearly visualize the types of environments where you would like to work and tailor your message to appeal to the decision makers from this environment, you are much more likely to be successful.

Also be aware that you may have collected a few career 'anchors' on your journey. Certain moments in time when you simply stopped moving forward or you became attached to a certain lifestyle and believed that life was better then and it will never be the same again. Recognize these and prioritize their importance in relation to your new career goals. Don't let these anchors keep you stuck!

Action 39: *To attract the right career, you need to be able to showcase your skills, knowledge, networks and attitude in a location where the right decision makers can find it. Your greatest need is someone else's opportunity*

7.1 Immediate Jobs

Right now you may be in a position where you need to find a job as quickly as possible. You could be in a desperate financial position, in a very hostile work environment or you may simply be sick and tired of the status quo. You may believe that adopting an attraction strategy will take too long. What you need to do first and foremost is open your mind to opportunity.

I would like to share the story of another one of my clients. He was a very capable man who had moved to a small city in a new country and he had been trying to find work for some time. His wife had already secured work and she was very happy in the role but he had started to believe that he would never find an opportunity because in his mind, there simply were not enough opportunities in this small city.

He was quite willing to leave the small city and move to a bigger city to find work because what he had been doing had not been working – he wasn't even getting interviews. If he chose to move to a bigger city, it would mean that he would be spending time away from his wife and that if he did secure a role in the bigger city, his wife would then have to give up her career and move to the big city and start all over again.

I should also mention that both the husband and the wife liked living in the small city and had created a nice circle of friends. However, the husband was quickly losing his confidence because he had been looking for work for quite some time and had not been successful at all.

I listened to all of his concerns and I found out that most of the information he had collected up to this point was anecdotes from ill-informed friends. I reminded him that most people are taught how to do a job but not how to find a job. We overhauled his LinkedIn Profile, his resume and his job search strategy and he secured the perfect role, aligned with his experience, within six weeks.

This was a far better outcome than his original idea of going to a bigger city. With the right strategy in place and an adjustment to his beliefs, he secured a new job quickly. It was also better for him to learn job search skills instead of applying for 'any job.'

I have often found that people become comfortable in an interim job and once they have become accustomed to a regular salary, they stay in that job beyond their immediate income requirement time and then become terribly frustrated over time. They plateau.

The point I am trying to reinforce here is that you need to remember that you must come from a place of well-informed research, willing contribution and shared value rather than desperate need. If you do secure an interview and you are desperate for any reason, the interviewer will be able to sense this (even if you give perfect answers) and you will probably miss out.

If you approach the job search process with an attitude of seeking the right fit, for both you and the enterprise, there will be a meeting of minds and you will be successful. There will be a fair exchange of shared benefits. Remember that the skills to do a job are different to the skills to find a job.

Action 40: *If you need an immediate job right now, remember that you need to have the right attitude, excellent job search skills, accurate information and the ability to effectively showcase your value before and during the job interview*

7.2 Survival Jobs And Means To An End Jobs

You may think that a 'survival' job is a job of last resort. I disagree. I have learnt a great deal from survival jobs. More importantly, they have enabled me to achieve my higher values.

My definition of a 'survival' job is a job that fits in and around the other demands of your life at that point in time. One of my clients had a job in a pizza shop. He was extremely embarrassed about this job because he was a fully qualified international engineer with a wealth of experience and he was completing a master's degree on a part time basis in a new country.

I explained to him that he should be extremely proud of this job. As he was new to the country, this job gave him local experience, an opportunity to improve his English, a reliable income, new friends and the ability to support himself. He was learning a range of very useful transferable skills. It turns out that he was able to make some excellent recommendations on how to improve the efficiency and profit of the business and his employer willingly gave him extra shifts so he could increase his earning capacity.

As he was so embarrassed about this 'survival' job, he did not include it on his resume or LinkedIn Profile. This meant that when decision makers looked at his profile, it looked as though he had been unemployed for some time and he did not have any local experience. I suggested that he needed to update his resume and LinkedIn Profile immediately and rather than just say 'Pizza Deliverer' and not provide any details about his experience, we compiled a very comprehensive summary of his tasks and achievements in this 'survival' job.

His whole outlook changed and sure enough, he secured an engineering job soon after. The pizza shop owner made it very clear that he would be welcome back at any time.

I have also heard stories about artists working in fast food stores so that they can earn a living so that they can follow their true passion. I call this a 'means to an end' job. You accept this type of work for a period of time knowing full well that it is only one step on the journey, not the entire road. You tolerate the role and make the most of your time there because you know that in the end, you are doing what you can to maintain your highest values.

Ultimately, if you find yourself in a 'survival' job or a 'means to an end' job, don't be disappointed. Look at the opportunities it is giving you. The flexibility, transferable skills, regular income, social interaction, security and even fun! No situation is ever hopeless – but if you can see how it is helping you live according to your values, you will be one step closer to attracting a better opportunity when you have developed your job search skills and implemented your career attraction strategies.

Action 41: *Identify the real value you are receiving from a survival or means to an end job and develop your job search skills and career attraction strategies so that your next job is more closely aligned to your values*

7.3 Aligned Jobs

If you are working in an aligned job, you will know how good it feels. How the combination of your skills, knowledge, experience and networks provides a good exchange between you and your employer. For some people, this is what they seek and nothing more.

What can traditionally happen is that someone who has a good skill level is recognized for that skill and then moved into or offered a supervisory or management role. As we all know, the skills required for management and leadership are different to technical skills. Some people are able to make the transition, others cannot. Most people who have worked for a few years will be able to tell you horror stories about bad managers who were technically very competent.

Some people choose to focus on increasing or maintaining their technical competency and they refuse an opportunity to move into a supervisory or management role. I encourage this approach if the decision is made consciously. I am usually disappointed if the person chooses not to grow because they don't want to deal with politics or perceived challenges. There are challenges in every aspect of life – and if you are willing to face them, you could be the person that changes the status quo – for the better – don't eliminate yourself from opportunities because of perceptions!

I made a technical versus managerial choice some years ago when I was offered my first promotion in the bank. At the time, I was a Customer Service Officer and I had direct contact with customers during banking hours. I was offered a 'Senior Customer Service Officer' role and this would mean sitting in the back of the office and supervising the team members and checking off reports. I politely declined the invitation and explained my reasons why – to me, working with people was much more important. This also meant that I forfeited a higher income.

Interestingly enough, a few short months later, I was offered an even better promotion – to the role of Training Officer. I was ecstatic and terrified at the same time. This was a huge acknowledgment of my customer service skills, a higher promotion than a Senior Customer Service Officer and it would mean that I would be developing a whole new range of skills with staff from across the state. After overcoming the shock and excitement and having a meaningful chat with my current supervisor (who encouraged me to take it), I accepted the role. I have never looked back and to this day, I am still teaching people.

This was a conscious choice where I chose to say 'no' to role that was not aligned and 'yes' to a role that was aligned. Isn't it amazing to see how the right opportunity was attracted to me by saying no to the wrong opportunity?

Action 42: *Be willing to say 'no' to the wrong opportunity and 'yes' to the right opportunity, even if you have to overcome an immediate benefit or potentially difficult challenges in the future. Make a conscious choice aligned with your values*

7.4 Next Step Up Jobs

You may be at a point where you are doing well in your current role but you are now looking for the next step up in your career. It could be a more technically competent role or a more senior role. It may be within the organization or in another organization.

Good employers are able to identify what needs to be done and they find the people who can do the work well. They either allow people to find the motivation from within or they inspire employees with the big picture. They enable individuals and teams to develop both personally and professionally.

A good team size is about seven people and a good tribe size is about 150 people (beyond that, it becomes a little more difficult for our brains to remember all of the details, connections and relevance of the individual people in the tribe). If you are assessing an organization and the opportunities available, you will need to look at how they reward their employees and how they recognize their contribution. By looking at these metrics in a logical fashion, you can compare opportunities objectively.

It is very important if you are wanting a new direction not to fall for the 'shiny object syndrome.' Where anything looks better than what you are currently doing or you see all the good parts and none of the bad parts. You still need to be discerning. A new opportunity does not need to be perfect, it rarely ever is completely perfect – but it does need to be aligned with your highest values.

For example, I simply cannot tolerate an autocratic environment. Where I am not able to contribute and participate effectively and efficiently. I am always interested in ways to do the same things just a little bit better. I can follow instructions and be a part of the team, but if I was told to do this, and only this, exactly like this, I would go nuts!

You also need to think about which stage you are at in your career voyage. Do you want to be an:

- employee
- specialist
- advisor
- manager
- leader
- owner
- investor
- entrepreneur

All of these roles are available within an organization. Will you have the opportunity to have this underlying need met in your next role? For example, entrepreneurs are willing to take risks – if you were applying for a role in an organization that was risk averse, you simply would not fit.

Now may also be a good time for you to think about some of the more discreet opportunities in a next step up role:

- incentives
- awards and rewards
- flexibility and work ethic
- autonomy or team work
- ability to specialize
- mentoring
- personal and professional development opportunities
- prestige or power within the organization or community
- travel and perks
- recognition of achievement
- reputation and authority development

- alignment value (short, medium or long term)
- commitment and loyalty required

You will need to think about how persistent you will need to be to secure the right fit. How you will need to persevere over time to work towards the right fit. Ultimately, employers are trying to attract, recruit and retain the best fit people. The most successful employers also wish you well on the next stage of your journey once your time with them has been completed and they make some effort towards keeping you in their alumni community.

Action 43: *When considering your 'next step up job,' look very carefully at the information you have gathered about the role and the organization and be discerning in the selection process. It needs to be an aligned fit and you need to assess multiple variables before accepting the role*

7.5 Job Identification Techniques

For some people, this will be the most important section in the whole book. You will want specific methodologies for finding a job so that you can choose your multiple concurrent strategies. I will always believe that the best way to source an opportunity is by referral and that a referral is usually attracted to you because your message is clear and within reach of the decision makers seeking that information.

I also know that creating this 'spider's web' can take a bit more time than seeing something and going for it. That said, I have seen some clients source amazing opportunities by being very clear about what they want and going directly after it and not stopping until they do get it!

In this section, I will reveal a variety of places where you can find the details of a present or future job vacancy:

- direct contact – call and ask!
- current organization employees
- organization intranets
- job advertisements on organization websites
- job advertisements on job aggregator websites
- job advertisements on classified job advertisement websites
- job advertisements on industry or profession websites
- job advertisements in printed publications including newspapers and specialty publications
- local community publications (groups, clubs, associations)
- recruitment company websites (temporary and permanent roles)
- recruitment marketing (like television campaigns for the defense force)
- landing pages (created for a specific purpose)
- labor hire and contract worker websites
- freelancing, outsourcing and project based websites

- social media profiles of organizations (like Facebook Pages, LinkedIn Career Pages etc)
- social referrals from people you know
- candidate database websites (where employers can search for potential candidates)
- video campaigns (for example https://www.youtube.com/watch?v=iTUUWOV4Vns)
- talent communities (where professionals aggregate)
- online forums
- past job applications

I would also like to remind you that some organizations rely on you contacting them rather than them contacting you! When I was in recruitment at the bank, we never advertised for applicants because enough applicants contacted us! When my son was underage and didn't have a resume, he simply telephoned people until someone said yes.

Even if you are unsuccessful at a job interview, you must always thank the people involved and let them know that you are willing to be considered for future jobs with the organization. I have several clients who have been offered an opportunity after they missed out with their first application.

You may also like to try working somewhere on a casual, temporary or part time basis and once the employer has seen you in action, you may find that a new role is created for you. There is a significant trend towards 'talent created roles' because the 'talent' has appeared (up to 20% of the yearly total of roles from one large retailer I spoke to).

Depending on your purpose and values, you can select a variety of the above job identification techniques. Once you have considered all of these options, you may find that there are even more out there that you can explore. Part of attracting the right career involves you finding out where the jobs are in the first place.

Action 44: *Select the five main job identification methods you believe will be most effective for finding the job you would like and review any others that may complement your selection. Actively use them*

_____

_____

_____

7.6 Job Application Techniques

There are some very important job application techniques that you need to consider when applying for jobs. Let's start by looking at some of the most common mistakes in written job applications (both the cover letter and resume):

- spelling and grammatical errors
- inconsistent grammar – current job should be in the present tense, a past job in the past tense
- interchanging person formatting (first person and third person)
- inconsistent and difficult to follow formatting
- too much formatting (which will conflict with Applicant Tracking Systems (ATS))
- missing information
- illogical order (some countries have a preference for experience, others prefer education)
- overuse of capitals (considered to be shouting)
- date gaps (these need to be explained)
- confusing information
- incoherent message
- irrelevant information (like personal data)
- template formatting (looks like you have a low level of digital literacy)
- too much jargon which a first level application assessor cannot understand

- stereotypical boring information (rather than interesting and relevant)
- cramped formatting (trying to squeeze too much information on to one page)
- including commercially sensitive information (convert numbers to percentages and make confidential information anonymous)
- If your job applications include these items, you are likely to repel opportunities, not attract opportunities.
- You need to remember that nowadays most people are going to view your information on a screen, not on a printed piece of paper. For this reason, it is important to make your job application screen friendly and:
- make sure that the information is tailored for the job you are applying for (ESSENTIAL)
- use dot points rather than long paragraphs as these are much easier to read and process
- use dot points of four words or less
- design your content for a screen rather than paper
- include all of your keywords, even if it makes your resume longer, so that you come up in the Applicant Tracking System (ATS) search results
- put your keywords from the job advertisement or description in both your cover letter and your resume
- make your content suitable for a mobile device, not just a desktop computer
- keep your formatting consistent and logical running down the screen rather than across it – include a brief description for every organization, particularly if they are not well known organizations so that the reader can gain some context from your experience
- make it easy to find information
- include relevant achievements with specifics (including details of opportunities offered to you in your roles, not just statistics of results)

- keep like information together so there is logic and flow in your application but also be aware of unconscious bias so be strategic in what you include and how you write it

- avoid writing anything that is not needed – you don't need to use the word 'Email' – just include the email address

- make it easy to scan – so people can quickly gather information by simply scanning rather than reading

- make sure the most important information appears first

- make sure that you include information that is relevant to the organization you will be working for (a detailed outline of your Japanese experience may be irrelevant to a new country but your transferable skills for the new organization in the new country are essential)

- tailor your application for the local market (don't rely on techniques from other locations)

- demonstrate your personal skills and motivation levels with interesting descriptions so that the application assessor can easily determine if you are a good fit

- if you don't have all of the skills required for the job, include a statement about being willing to learn new skills in your own time and being willing to work with a mentor

- go the extra mile and personalize your application as much as possible (for example, include the name of the decision maker you are sending it to, the organization name and street address on the cover letter)

- don't ever lie (but you can massage the truth and present information in a more attractive manner)

If the job application is aligned with the job, you are much more likely to secure an interview. If you miss out after the interview, it is usually because you are not the right cultural fit.

Remember that most decision makers will also do an internet search before they consider you for an interview and will definitely do an internet search before they offer you the job. If you have inappropriate information accessible on websites, social media etc, be warned! Now is the time to remove this content from online platforms. Do not rely on security settings to protect you.

Action 45: *If you provide a tailor made job application for each job you apply for, you are much more likely to attract the right opportunity. You also need to make sure that your application is screen friendly*

7.7 Job Application Persistence Techniques

If you are applying for jobs and looking for ways to attract the right job, it is important for you to realize that it is not just a process of hoping for the right job or allowing it to manifest automatically.

Here are a few suggestions for you to consider to make sure that the right job comes to you:

- follow up your applications, by email, direct message, phone, visit

- thank everyone along the way, even when you get a no

- request meetings – if the person cannot communicate now, make a time for later

- source encouragement – so even when you miss out, someone is still encouraging you to keep going – persistence works!

- account manage the process – prepare your own job application spreadsheet or database so that you can document all of the applications and outcomes and schedule your follow ups

- submit a printed application as well as an electronic application – it will make you stand out

- send a copy of the application to other people within the firm to let them know how interested you really are about the role (but be polite)

- make sure you are always using multiple concurrent strategies – one technique alone is never enough

- always work on building your network, your personal profile (offline and online) and your level of trust and authority in your niche – even if you miss out on a particular role, there are still gains you can make along the way and these can help you in the future

- be polite at ALL times. No matter how frustrated you become, always smile, say thank you and do not appear bitter or angry. Bad behavior is likely to be remembered

- allocate a regular time commitment – as stated before, up to two hours per day, five days per week

- seek feedback when you can so that you can learn more from the process. If you reflect on your performance, ask yourself what has worked well and what could be improved. Make some decisions and carry out new actions

- be willing to back yourself. Yes, it takes time and money to complete applications, attend interviews and follow up and you may ask yourself why bother? However, if you want to move forward, you have to do whatever works and you won't know what works until you have hindsight – and you only get hindsight after you have done it!

Action 46: *If you are truly genuine in your desire to attract the right job opportunity, you will need to be extremely persistent and there are many tasks that you will need to complete. Be courageous and keep going*

7.8 Job Interview Techniques

If your job applications are leading to interviews, you are on the road to success. However, very few people score an interview for every job application they make. If you can secure one job interview from every 10 tailor made job applications, you are doing very well. If you are making hundreds of job applications and not getting any interviews, you need to review your job application process entirely.

If you have secured a job interview, you can partly assume that your job application provides enough information for you to be considered for the role. If you find out after the interview that you didn't get the job because you 'don't have any local experience,' this is simply a 'safe' answer where the decision maker does not reveal the real reason for not hiring you – if you didn't have the right experience, why did they bother interviewing you? You would have told them the location of your experience in your job application.

When I was in recruitment, it used to annoy me when my supervisor would ask me to always provide the organization with three potential candidates for interviewing by the organization for each role. In my view, my job was to help the organization find the best candidate for the role and to save them time and money. If I am their trusted advisor, in theory I should be able to interview all of the applicants (by phone or in person) and then they only need to interview the best possible candidates. If that means interviewing just one person, then so be it – why waste two other candidate's time?

When I hear that organizations have an interview panel of three or more staff and they are going to personally interview more than three candidates for one job, I instantly know that their recruitment processes are poor. That is four people's time for at least four hours and a huge time and expense cost for everyone involved. Any additional candidates after the first three should be eliminated by some other process (normally a phone interview).

This is also what makes looking for a job very frustrating for you! If you also add in phone interviews, virtual online interviews, group interviews, second stage interviews, you can quickly see how many hours are potentially wasted looking for a new job. If you go through all of this and miss out on a job that you really like, it can be extremely frustrating.

I remember when I first moved interstate. I was fortunate to secure several interviews within six weeks, but every time, they would tell me that I had missed out and most of the time, they would tell me I had come 'second.' I deduced that this was the same as coming last – I still did not get the job.

I was becoming very despondent but I realized that wouldn't help, so I decided to change my outlook. I realized that if I was missing out, it was because I wasn't the right fit and I may be appearing 'desperate' to get work and be trying too hard to convince them of my value. So I changed my approach. The next interview I went to was entirely different.

This time I asked them for more information about their company, the career opportunities, how long the other staff had been there and so on. This created a 'reverse psychology' effect – if they didn't make a decision about me now, then they would miss out because I was someone focused on the best exchange of value for me and the organization. Believe it or not, they offered me three jobs on the spot. I took the best one!

There are many very subtle nuances that can affect the outcome of a job interview. Ultimately what you must accept is that if you did not get the job, something better will be coming along, you and the organization were not the right fit at the right time.

There are some things that you can do to improve your chances in a job interview:

- dress appropriately and if in doubt, dress more formally but not in cultural type clothing – in work type clothing – your personal appearance can be a critical factor as so many people rely on first impressions (even when they say they don't)
- arrive early in a relaxed state (allowing for any security or entry procedures)
- make sure you have eaten, had a drink and been to the toilet so you can perform at your best
- check yourself in the mirror to make sure that you look okay and you don't have food stuck in your teeth
- smile frequently and shake hands or perform the local greeting customs
- listen carefully to the questions and answer them – do not try and evaluate your answers as you give them
- go with the flow – if they want to take the conversation in a different direction, you do not need to insist on discussing your capabilities
- maintain the appropriate amount of eye contact and be aware of your body language and local customs
- be polite and allow the conversation to flow naturally (don't take over)
- be aware of the personality types of the people in the interview and be respectful – not too overbearing or too meek – if in doubt, try and align your behavior with theirs
- match the pace of the interview – not too fast or too slow
- discuss the most relevant pieces of information – give relevant examples, not grandiose statements that give them the impression you will move on if a better opportunity comes along
- be realistic about your salary or financial package expectations. Most interviewers feel uncomfortable if you initiate this discussion but you can subtly ask by saying 'can you give me any more specific details about this job opportunity?'

- be willing to ask if there is an opportunity to meet and discuss the details of the job after three months in the role (particularly if it is a sideways move or a role with a lower salary)

- only share information that you are allowed to share (do not reveal confidential information from your past)

- do not criticize anyone else – if you say something negative about someone else, a person will believe that one day, you will say something negative about them

- local laws may prevent certain questions from being asked (like any personal needs you may have outside the office – caring responsibilities etc). It is up to you to decide how you will handle questions about these matters. If you decide not to reveal this information and it is within your legal rights, you may choose to say 'I believe that according to local laws, I am not required to answer that question'

- if you are asked a question and you don't know the answer, you can say that although you currently don't know how to answer the question, you are willing to undertake further study or training in the future, in your own time if necessary

- if you are aware that you simply don't connect at any level, you must still be polite and respectful and treat the exercise as a learning experience. It may be possible to ask the person if they have any advice or recommendations for you as this could lead to a good referral

- be authentic – if you pretend in the interview, you won't necessarily be able to keep up the acting in the job and it won't work out for either of you

- if you think you are going to miss out because they are just going through a formality, again, recognize that you are gaining interview experience and the more interviews you get, the closer you are to securing a job

When it is all over, do not beat yourself up and worry. You did the best you could at the time. Review and reflect and think about what changes you could make next time.

Some people like interviews, others don't. If interviews are your weakest point, try and work out ways to meet people more naturally rather than through the formal interview process.

My last formal job interview was for a job with a very high profile professional association and the woman asked me questions that were actually impossible to answer. For example – she asked me whether I would prefer to work full time for three months or part time for six months. In my case, either option fitted in with my current lifestyle and business commitments but she insisted that I make a choice. I can't even remember which one I picked. I decided at that point that I would stop going for 'normal jobs' – I obviously wasn't cut out to be locked up in the one organization and follow her rules! I did not get the job.

However, I have easily secured many other casual interesting and challenging roles ever since and I have worked when it suits me. Most of these roles have been secured without a formal job interview – just a meeting where we agree on terms.

Another person I knew turned up at an interview and was asked three job related questions. He then spent the next hour talking about fishing with his interviewers. He got the job. There is not always a standard 'formula' for job interview success – so you need to be flexible in your approach.

Action 47: *Learn the basic principles of job interviews and learn new skills from each job interview that you attend. See every interview as an opportunity to learn and grow and one step closer to your job goal*

7.9 Job Interview Follow Up Techniques

Once you have been through the job interview, it is time to follow up. You have several alternatives:

- personalized email with some descriptive feedback
- personal phone call
- hand written card or note sent in the post
- direct SMS message by phone
- direct message via an online platform
- sending an appropriate gift (within local laws and customs)

When you are sending this message, you need to include

- a statement that says 'thank you for the opportunity of attending an interview on Monday' (you may also like to say 'with Rachel Jones and Simon Sharpe')
- some details that were discussed in the interview about the role 'the role is very appealing to me because I am particularly interested in……'
- some specific feedback about the interviewer/s 'I appreciated the friendly atmosphere and extra information shared in the interview'
- some specific information from you 'it was also interesting to hear about your organizations plans for the future and the opportunities that will be coming up'
- a polite thank you once again and a call to action 'once again, I would like to thank you for your time and I look forward to hearing from you in the future. If for any reason I am unsuccessful in relation to this role, I would like to be considered for other opportunities you hear about that are related to my skills and experience'
- sign off 'Yours sincerely,….'

I cannot express how important it is to say THANK YOU at every available opportunity. I realize that most of the people in the interview process will be paid for their time and you will not be paid for your time. That is irrelevant. You need to be polite and courteous as you are much more likely to be remembered and referred to an opportunity that is aligned if you are unsuccessful with this opportunity.

A job interview is also an opportunity to build your reputation, for people to remember you and for them to share your information. It could lead to the perfect referral. It may not seem like it at the time, but no time is ever wasted.

Action 48: *Follow up after every job interview and always make sure that you include a message of thanks and a call to action for the future*

7.10 Accepting A Job Offer

If you are going through the process of applying for several jobs at once, there is a very real chance that you will be offered several jobs at a similar time. You then need to make a decision about which job to take!

I usually suggest that before you accept any offer, you request a copy of the offer in writing. It doesn't need to arrive in the post, but some basic details do need to be confirmed so that you can make an informed choice. If the organization is not prepared to put the offer in writing, I would be very suspicious!

I often encourage people to give themselves some time to think about the offer rather than say 'yes' immediately. Not always, but sometimes. If you have not read the offer in detail, you may be rushing things. You may also want some time to go over the offer in more detail with someone else. You may even want to negotiate a better offer, either before you start or three months after commencement.

If you are waiting to hear back from another role, you may also want to hear the outcome from that opportunity before you accept the current opportunity.

If you decide to accept a job offer, you can do so personally and in writing.

If you accept an offer and a better offer comes along, you will need to decide what to do – both professionally and ethically. If you have decided to decline the first offer and accept the second offer, once the second offer has been fully confirmed, you need to contact the first offer organization as soon as practicable and be prepared for any penalties that may be incurred. You must also sincerely apologize for any inconvenience.

Once you have accepted a job offer, you MUST complete all of the necessary administration as quickly as possible. You need to finalize matters from your current role too if you are changing jobs.

You need to be well prepared for your first day in the new role and be able to arrive on time with everything that you need to perform your duties. It is important for you to clarify any specific work and safety requirements on day one. You also need to ask for details if you need further information (some tragic accidents have occurred because people were reluctant to ask questions). You may also need to sign certain policy and employment documentation.

I encourage you to continually find out information about how things work in your new role. I also encourage you to be realistic about your expectations in the new role – you cannot expect to be perfect in the job on the first day, regardless of how much experience you have. In my view, it takes around six months to become unconsciously competent in a new role. So please, be kind to yourself and ask for help if you need it.

Most work colleagues know that it will take some time to perform at your best when you are in a new role – and if you are polite and friendly, they will probably offer some extra assistance. If you are rude and arrogant and try and do everything on your own in your own way, you could easily lose the job.

Action 49: *Make sure that you receive your job offer in writing and give yourself time to review the offer, make a decision and complete any administration. Once accepted, make sure that you are fully prepared to start the new role on day one*

8. Business Attraction Tips And Techniques

Businesses exist because people see a value and pay for what the business provides. The more value a business offers, the more business they attract. The value determines how the business generates profit, leverage determines how the volume of business is multiplied (usually via some form of replication and it is usually cheapest if the replication is automatic). Some businesses focus on the margin, others focus on mystery. The ultimate value proposition is either real or perceived.

Action 50: *Business provides a value exchange and to attract more business, provide more value*

8.1 Real Value In Business

Less than two years ago, a small green grocer set up shop in a small strip of suburban shops a few kilometers from where I live. He started selling green groceries at prices I hadn't seen in more than 20 years. In fact on some occasions when I went there, he was selling goods for one cent per kilogram (which basically means that the first five kilograms are free as the smallest coin in our currency here is five cents).

I could not believe how this green grocer could possibly survive with such cheap prices! Now, whenever I go past this shop there is always a crowd there buying goods and there are several people waiting in a queue to be served.

Anyway, about six months after the business had started, I asked the Green Grocer how he could offer such cheap prices. It was a slightly sad story. He had previously had three stores across the city but his marriage had broken down and he had to sell the three stores and he only had enough money to set up one store.

However, what he did keep was the excellent buying arrangements he had built up over the years with his fruit and vegetable suppliers. His produce is definitely 'second grade' but when it is so cheap, the customers are willing to sacrifice some quality. To make sure he earns a living, he works on a high volume basis not a high profit margin basis.

What I also like about his business is that he is encouraging people to eat healthy food – because it is so affordable! He is also helping local people meet each other whilst they are out shopping locally. He is also supporting at least eight other employees and is required by local laws to pay the correct salaries.

In my view, he has an impressive business attraction strategy – because he offers so much value and the excitement of unexpected and welcome surprises. He has the potential to leverage his business further if he sets up additional stores once he has enough equity in this store.

If you are planning to go into your own business, or you already have your own business, you need to be both proactive and realistic. I have seen some of the best businesses fail and the worst businesses succeed – so I believe that you need to start out with the view that there is definitely no guarantee with any business opportunity – but your attitude can make the world of difference.

In my view, there are some essential components of a good quality value proposition and a sustainable business:

- there is a reliable market available (locally or internationally)
- there is real value in the product or service
- the business is prepared for a volatile environment and is not over-exposed in any area
- customers can go on a value ladder journey either before a big ticket item sale or increase their spend with several transactions over time
- the business owners can source reliable data from business operations and customer feedback and adjust their business accordingly
- the business owners are constantly willing to learn and grow and remain relevant to their current and future customers
- the business owners are always interested in innovation – but they also understand the importance of not running after 'shiny object' ideas that may detract from the viability of the business

- where possible, processes are automated to save time and effort
- they are aware of market conditions
- they understand cash flow and how important it is to keep it flowing
- they effectively manage their income and expenses and look for trends
- they are willing to plan, test and trial before making expensive decisions
- they manage their time and health

It is important to look at all of these variables and make a decision as to whether or not you are really suitable for life in business. I say this because some people go straight from a job into a business that they have purchased after receiving a financial payout from a previous job and then they wonder why it isn't the same as being in a job.

If you are at the point of assessing a business opportunity, you need to consider all of these variables before looking at how you will attract business. For example, if the market for your goods or services has almost vanished (e.g. fax machines), you would be wise to undertake further research before starting a business. If you have trouble disciplining yourself with either time or money, you will not necessarily have a manager telling you what to do in your own business. These issues can detract from your ability to attract business.

Action 51: *Before you invest in a business (either a start-up or an existing business), assess the real value that the products or services provide to customers and make sure that there is a sustainable market of potential customers that you can attract. Be aware of basic business sustainability principles*

8.2 Perceived Value In Business

Just as people have a perceived value when being considered as a candidate for a career, there is also perceived value in business. It can come from the products and services or it can come from the way that these products and services are delivered.

Personally, I cannot ever imagine paying over $1,000 for a designer label hand bag – I do not see any value in that purchase – but for some people, who like the style, quality and prestige that comes with the hand bag, $1,000 could be a bargain price!

Alternatively, you may have a favorite restaurant that you like to go to on a regular basis. You like it because they make a particular type of food exactly how you like it and you find the staff friendly and cheerful. But you also know that at any time, a fancy new restaurant will open up and all of sudden, crowds will flock to the new venue, queue for a table and book months in advance for the opportunity to enjoy the new venue. They may still have an a la carte menu with a similar range of dining choices, but their perceived value attracts extra business.

The amount of perceived value can be manipulated with clever marketing, public relations and social media. It can be changed both positively and negatively. Just the right amount can be difficult to achieve and many businesses have suffered due to bad perceptions that they could not overcome. This is why I like to encourage business owners to have a risk mitigation strategy.

This involves having enough good information out in the marketplace so that if any bad information surfaces, it has less of an impact. It also means responding appropriately – and if you do it particularly well, you can actually end up creating a fantastic perception.

There are some general perceptions that business owners can accept responsibility for and manage so that they can increase their perceived value:

- reasonable website and/or store front
- reliable and efficient service (speed is becoming extremely important)
- quality of customer service (online or in person)
- consistency of feedback and follow up
- ability to adapt to changing market needs
- level of innovation and relevancy
- record of achievements (internally and externally)

What I am also noticing is that online content is having a significant effect on perceived value. Ratings, reviews, social media dialogue and responses to that dialogue, press coverage etc are becoming very important. I believe that every business owner should be aware of these opportunities, so they will be discussed in detail in this book.

If you want to have a business that successfully attracts the right customers, you need to be concerned about your real value and your perceived value. As a matter of interest, products and services that are considered to be 'high end' generally sell better – so it is worth thinking about ways you can increase your perceived value.

Action 52: *Business owners need to understand how they can influence the perceived value in their products and services and how they will manage the situation if a bad perception is created*

8.3 Referral Value In Business

For as long as anyone can remember, one of the best ways to attract business is via referral – also known as word of mouth. This is what happens when one person asks another person, where should I go to purchase a product or service?

In days gone by when people did not travel very far, it was easy to share information around a community. Now there are so many messages being sent all the time that many people are starting to become overwhelmed by all of the choices and they are looking for ways to shortcut the selection process – just the same way as the brain decides which information to absorb as we go about our daily living.

When there were fewer information distribution channels, just billboards, newspapers, magazines, directories and the radio, it was fairly easy to reach your ideal customer – just pick which publication they were consuming and advertise there!

Nowadays the marketplace is a LOT noisier. We have free to air and pay television, dynamic billboards, podcasts, vodcasts, social media, internet searches, computers, tablets, mobile devices, apps, neon signs and more! What is also happening is that more and more market segments have been created and more and more customers are seeking (or receiving and becoming accustomed to), a personalized experience.

For example, when a relative of mine was buying a car, they were using their mobile device to compare and select a finance product. Sure enough, their Facebook feed soon filled up with sponsored advertisements from finance companies!

With this significant shift in personalized buying, business needs to adapt.

For the most part, people do business with people. This is why I always encourage business owners to maintain both face to face and online business marketing strategies.

People prefer experiences to explanations and they also like to feel as if they are receiving good advice if they go out and seek advice. This good advice can come from a person or an authorized, reputable, credible and reliable brand.

If we think about some of the biggest online traders – Amazon, Alibaba and eBay, they have managed to create an environment where the customer feels as if their expectations will be met – even though the customer never meets anyone from the online store. The information has been collated in such a way that the customer can gather the information they need to make a buying decision and the customer service and returns policy means that the customer has a right of recall if the planned purchase is not successful.

These businesses have also been particularly good at generating upsells. Upsells are good because the customer is already in buying mode and the trader can simply leverage an additional opportunity from a warm prospect.

Understanding the cycle of customers is also important. A traditional marketing funnel would take people from a large sized cold prospect group to the medium sized warm prospect group and finally into the small sized hot prospect group and then at a critical moment in time, they would become a customer. This process is sometimes abbreviated to Suspect, Prospect, Client.

Nowadays, people more typically go from the decision to buy a product or service, to researching and verifying their choice and then purchasing the product or service. People are essentially being driven to purchase from a transaction mode rather than an advertising mode.

They are also willing to pay when they believe that they will receive value.

Some business owners attempt to generate pre-awareness of a product or service, by planting a seed of an idea and then generating more detailed awareness over time. This helps create a greater interest and consideration for the product or service. It also helps with creating that buying decision in the first place and as the customer is already well informed, speeds up the process from conversion to commitment.

Essentially, these business owners start by building traffic, generating engagement and finally, securing a sale. In this scenario, business needs to carefully monitor the cost of attracting the traffic and then measuring the cost of converting that traffic into paying customers.

We can be quite sure that as our world changes, the way that businesses attract referrals will also change. I believe that the concept of a referral has lasted for so long because it has an element of trust involved and people like to believe others. Savvy shoppers also know that trust alone is not enough, they need to verify the information they collect before they make a purchase.

Action 53: *Businesses need to choose the best ways to continually attract referrals to their business by making sure that there is an interest in the product or service, a group of people who can easily find and verify the product or service and then feel comfortable paying the set price. The methodology for sourcing these referrals will continue to change over time*

8.4 Clarity Value In Business

In the noisy world of business today, there is one principle that stands above the rest. Clarity. If you are going to succeed, you must have the ability to make it very clear as to what products or services you are offering, you need to capture that audience and you need to convert it into a sale.

You also need to be able to find the customers who need your product or service the most. If you are absolutely crystal clear about who these people are and there is a reasonable demand from these people (and not too many competitors), then you have a business.

Many new business owners are so excited by their product or service, they mistakenly believe that EVERYONE will want what they have to offer. They are wrong.

Many new business owners also believe that they need to compete against their competitors. In one sense they do, but in many others, they do not. It is my genuine belief that there is enough abundance in the world for everyone and that if you offer a service, some people will prefer to use your service and other people will prefer to use someone else's service. If you have a product, the same principle applies – particularly if price or location is a factor in the decision making process.

Let me share an example. I am an Independent LinkedIn Specialist and I help people use LinkedIn for their purpose. I adopt a training approach as I believe that the individual person or enterprise needs to understand the platform before they can really gain maximum value. So I like to actively engage and teach my clients and select the most appropriate recommendations for their purpose.

Other LinkedIn Specialists have a different approach. They may concentrate on writing the content of a LinkedIn Profile or try and automate a sales process (which I absolutely hate because in most cases they are spamming people). If I meet someone who wants sales scripts and process driven sales, I politely decline their business – this is not aligned with my philosophy. I am very clear about the type of clients I want to serve.

By being absolutely clear about the service I offer, I have created an attraction strategy that pulls in exactly the type of clients I like to work with. I have also been able to refer any non-congruent potential clients to other LinkedIn Specialists. I also willingly share what I know with other LinkedIn Specialists and the beauty of this process is that they then return the favor and refer their non-congruent clients to me!

The same principle can apply to products. Let's think about the local corner store. We all know that they do not always offer the same price for their products as a major chain of stores and yet as customers, we willingly pay that little bit extra because we appreciate the convenience, the personal service or even just the principle of supporting a small business owner rather than a multi-millionaire CEO who travels by helicopter! Some of us also believe that by spending our money locally, we keep the money in our local community and we keep that business open. Whenever possible, I buy my products close to home.

Some local stores have felt the competition of online stores and I have also worked out a way around this issue so that I can still support my local small businesses. Last year I needed a new washing machine as my old washing machine was slowly dying after 20 years of very brutal loyal service. Instead of 'window shopping' in a retail store and then buying online, I went window shopping online and then contacted my local store and asked if they would be able to offer a similar price. They did without any hesitation and my washing machine was promptly delivered the next day – how good is that? What was even more exciting was that this local store also had a policy of donating a percentage of every sale back to the local community, so I was able to select a community group from their list and they received a small donation on my behalf (at no extra cost to me).

Did you also know that for many business owners, their business is actually a mirror of themselves? If they are disorganized and unsure personally, then their business comes across as disorganized and unsure. If they are clear, focused and friendly, then their business comes across as clear, focused and friendly. If you know that your business is not going in the direction you want, then I encourage you to find someone who can help you gain clarity – preferably someone who has their own clarity and experience from their own business and has 'walked the talk' – not just a 'weekend course' coach who has great quotes to share.

Action 54: *Whether you are about to start a business or continue in an existing business, make sure that you are very clear about why you are in business, how you will do it and who you will serve – this clarity will attract opportunity, confusion will drive customers away*

8.5 Reciprocity Value In Business

There is a great deal of natural reciprocity in business. Suppliers work with Wholesalers and they work with Retailers and each group in the chain has a level of reciprocity to the other. If the Retailer runs a bad business, this can affect both the Supplier and the Wholesaler.

Strategic alliances with other businesses that share the same customer base but offer different products and services can be extremely powerful and help build a market very quickly. Preferred supplier arrangements, tenders and contracts can also be used to make sure that both parties keep their side of the deal.

In the past, many businesses have kept their operations a secret – even from their own employees! Businesses have also been reluctant to 'share the love' when an oversupply of demand has occurred. The concept of working in partnership with another business, even at the 'white label' level, may have been refused.

However, in the 'social' economy where so much demand is driven by a business's algorithmic performance, the more closely your business is connected to your industry and profession, the more likely it is to perform well in internet search results. The more websites that are linked, the more network connections established (like on LinkedIn) and the more content that is shared (online or offline), the greater the chance of business success.

Let's look at a couple of ways you can build reciprocal value in business:

- congratulate your competitors publicly when they receive noteworthy recognition (they will be impressed by your generosity)
- refer your unsuitable clients to competitor businesses (they will appreciate a free referral)
- work with closely aligned businesses (see what you can outsource so you can increase your own business efficiency)
- find ways to work on joint projects (perhaps the project is too big for you – but if you partner with a larger business, it could work)
- always go back to anyone who has given you a referral or an opportunity and say thank you
- be friendly when you see competitors in person and be polite and friendly at all times – if they are difficult, still be polite and friendly
- be willing to introduce your competitors to others (just because you cannot accept an opportunity, don't keep it a

secret from your competitors – if you refer first and they do not appreciate the opportunity, you know not to do it again for that business but you can still refer to other businesses. If the business does appreciate the offer, you stand to gain even more opportunities in the future)

- consider sharing good quality content publicly – if you are seen to acknowledge good content, this shows that you can appreciate good quality and a level playing field

- systemize some business practices so that you can automate the reciprocal value opportunity (for example, you could set up a Google Alert on your competitor's business name and then see what they are doing that you can acknowledge)

If you are from the 'old school' of business, you are probably thinking right now that I am crazy! However, you do not have to look very far to see how new business models are constantly appearing.

I have spent many years working on a voluntary basis for community groups that have had their basic financial needs met via a philanthropic grant or government funding. This model is quickly disappearing and in its place, we have social entrepreneurship – where talented individuals or groups come together and decide how they can fund their own form of social change or justice through sustainable activities that cover the cost of their operations.

We can also see how new electronic platforms have transformed the way that we share photos, keep in touch with our friends and find employment. The current level of business disruption appears to be increasing exponentially. This means that our approach to business also needs to change. If we try and bunker down and fight the good fight and stick with the old principles of business, we have the very real potential of becoming obsolete. We must not throw everything out either as many 'old' formulas do still work. Building the reciprocal value of your business can be a creative way to attract new business opportunities.

Action 55: *Although it may be uncomfortable at first, be willing to share business opportunities on a reciprocal basis as it can be a great tool for increasing your ability to attract new business opportunities*

8.6 Uncertainty Value In Business

You may be wondering how you can gain value with both clarity and uncertainty in business! Clarity helps you decide what to do. Uncertainty reminds you to keep doing things even when you are not exactly sure what you should be doing!

I am certain that there will always be uncertainty. This means that we need to be comfortable with uncertainty. When faced with difficult decisions, Richard Branson suggests that we need to look at the situation and ask ourselves "What is the absolute worst thing that could happen?" We then need to ask ourselves "If the absolute worst thing did happen, how would I cope?" This process can help you make a decision.

You may choose a different strategy. For example, you could evaluate what you do know and then weigh up the potential risks or you could set some essential criteria that needs to be satisfied first. Whichever method you choose, make sure it works for you – or at least, find ways to cope with the consequences! Try not to worry too much, even the worst decisions with the worst consequences have hidden blessings.

If you find decision making a little difficult, remember that you are making decisions all of the time. What time to get up in the morning, what to wear or eat, where to go, etc. Business decisions are just additional decisions, not entirely new, unique and difficult decisions.

You may have also noticed that some of your previous decisions may have felt wrong at the time, but with the benefit of hindsight, you realize that they were actually the catalyst for a wonderful opportunity. You may have had something go terribly wrong right at the last moment, just before you were about to achieve success (but you still overcame the issue and triumphed). Or you may have realized that some of your best decisions were made when you didn't know all of the facts but you backed yourself and your abilities and went with a decision that felt right (in your head, heart or stomach) and it turned out to be a wonderful success.

All I am suggesting is that if you are going to attract new business, you need to be willing to work in an uncertain environment. The rate of change to the way we are living and working is increasing at an exponential rate. We are no longer in a society facing digital disruption, we are actually living in a digital era.

Action 56: *Be willing to make decisions in an uncertain environment. Develop your own decision making strategy and find ways to cope with consequences. Remember that even the worst situations have hidden blessings*

8.7 Pricing Value In Business

How much are you worth? How much are your products and services worth? Do you charge a price or do you exchange value? Do you calculate fixed and variable costs and add in a profit margin or do you calculate what sort of return needs to be generated and charge an appropriate percentage?

Traditional business models have essentially relied on costing methods for pricing. Today's prices reflect a myriad of variables. Let's look at a common example, accountancy services.

In the past, a business would employ a bookkeeper and an accountant to take care of financial matters. The bookkeeper would manually enter transactions in some form of register and the accountant would review these transactions and make suggestions to the business owner so that they could minimize their tax payments, increase their profits and improve their business performance.

Now, a business can have most of their transactions automatically recorded in their accounting system when the transaction occurs and the system can also generate reports and interpret the results. The traditional services provided by an accounting firm were largely time bound, now they are value bound.

However, an accounting practice still needs to pay for up to date computer systems, business operation costs and professional development. Whilst the tasks that have previously taken many hours to complete can probably be completed in just a few hours, the role of the accountant is still extremely important in the life of a business, especially if the business owner does not want to allocate the time to keep up to date with all of the changes in the industry.

The business cannot expect the accountant to do all of the work on a time cost basis unless it is a very high time cost basis. The business and the accountant need to come to a shared agreement as to what is a fair exchange based on the value of the service. For example, if the accountant is able to save the business $100,000 per year, surely the business owner cannot expect to receive this value for $100 simply because the advice was collected in 15 minutes. The business owner should be grateful that it only took 15 minutes to find that saving!

Attracting opportunity, as I have said previously, relies on a fair exchange. If necessary, review your own pricing models. You may actually find that you are not charging enough for the value you offer. The time it takes to manufacture a hand-made item that sells for just $100 could equate to just $2 an hour after the cost of materials is taken from the sale price. Likewise, some value is intangible or priceless. For some people, the pleasure they receive from a creative experience or artwork is priceless, so even though the time and cost to produce the item may only be $1,000, the value and pleasure that lasts a lifetime could be in excess of $100,000 – in that case, a reasonable sale price could easily be $10,000.

These examples also explain why 'bargain hunters' are motivated to make 'bargain purchases.' In their mind, if they only pay $10 for an item and they receive $1,000 in value, they are very grateful – they have attracted a value much higher than the purchase price.

Action 57: *Look at your business and who you exchange value with and look at ways to identify the total value that you share. Calculate any payment exchanges based on the value of your exchange rather than simply the time and costs of your exchange*

8.8 Human Value in Business

The value provided by business owners, employees, contractors, advisers, alliance partners etc is a key component of most businesses. The way that these people provide their service is also changing. Thanks to technology, many of these people do not need to be physically located at the business premises. They may be able to work close by or on the other side of the world. They may choose to work full time, part time, casually or be on call 24 hours a day.

In the past, the people in a business were called 'personnel.' This suggests to me individual people. Now, they are more likely to be called 'human resources' – in other words, another part of the business that drives output or results. This 'title' is likely to change again in the future.

What is also changing is how work is done and the mix of the people who do that work. There is a lot more diversity in business – across culture, ability, gender, faith, country of origin etc and also the actual workflow. Some employees and associates of the business are choosing to work part time by choice (even those not raising children and still under the age of 30). Some people appreciate the ability to work longer days for three days and not at all on two days. Businesses find it very convenient to employ staff on an hourly basis based on demand rather than at fixed times on fixed days.

Significant concerns have been raised about the reduction in employment opportunities and the ability of people to keep up to date with all of the technological changes. There has been an almost paranoid fear developing that robots will take over every aspect of our daily lives and all of the job opportunities.

Business owners need to embrace the new reliable technologies as they come along and incorporate them into the business in an appropriate way. I recently went to a local restaurant that serves pizza and Italian food. Apparently, the premises look exactly the same as they did more than 10 years ago. Most of the people who go there have been going there for many years because they like the taste of the food and the friendly service of the well-known staff members.

However, technology and business improvements have still changed this business over time. They have had to create a website so that any potential new customers can easily find them on their computer or phone. They need to offer an online ordering service so that customers can collect their takeaway food (or have it delivered) without making a phone call. Their cash register and accounting systems have changed. Sure, robots could take over the pizza making process, but part of the experience of going to this restaurant is seeing the people who are there and engaging in chit-chat.

People within a business and customers are all expecting more now than they ever have in the past. Customers see new ideas in other businesses and they then expect to see the same improvements across the industry or profession.

Understanding the human and technological value in your business will help you attract the right people. Mass sackings have occurred in various industries because the nature of the work has changed so significantly. The people who will remain employable are the people who are willing to constantly learn and grow over time. The people who are the most adaptable to the changing circumstances will be the survivors. Whilst language literacy has been a key to economic empowerment in the past, digital literacy will be the key to a life well lived in the future. We all need to adopt a 'learning' approach to life.

Action 58: *Every person associated with a business is expecting more now than they have in the past. The businesses and the people that will attract the best opportunities are the people who are willing to constantly learn, grow and adapt to the changing environment*

8.9 Asset Value In Business

When you start out in business, you are not necessarily thinking about the day you will leave the business – but every successful entrepreneur knows from the beginning that they should be planning their exit strategy.

There are various alternatives – for example, you could just close the business and cease trading. However, what you will probably want to do is sell the business or pass it on to someone else at a time of your choosing.

So from the beginning, you need to build both the cash flow of the business as well as the asset value of the business. If you are able to start a business with a low investment (and there are many low cost ways to start a business nowadays and grow organically without seed funding, particularly if you utilize the sharing economy), you will probably be starting without any significant assets. If you want to grow the business, you will need to develop your assets and a sustainable revenue.

So from day one, you need to start recording your assets. If you are a digital or service based business, you may feel that this is difficult to do – but every new subscriber, member, follower, connection, friend etc on the various platforms enables your enterprise to keep attracting business.

There are various assets in every business. Fixed assets (like the premises if you own them), current assets (like your stock levels) and in today's world, there are also digital assets. I believe that valuing these assets will be a very important part of determining the value of a business in the future.

Here is a quick example. A real estate business can help people sell their home or they can manage a property on behalf of a landlord so that a tenant can live in the property. Attracting a prospective property seller is usually a 'one-time' transaction and in many cases – after the property has been sold, the relationship with the real estate agent ends.

On the other hand, a landlord relationship can last for as long as they keep the investment property and the revenue can occur every month for years. This means that the one original transaction leads to ongoing income. This is also the reason why most real estate agencies that focus on selling properties have a very low asset value and real estate agencies that have a large number of long term properties under management will have a high asset value.

If the real estate agency also has a high traffic website, a large mailing list, significant numbers of subscribers, members, followers, connections, friends etc on online platforms that regularly generates business referrals, then they can increase the overall asset value of the business and the sale price of the business.

Whilst you are recording the increase in the digital asset value of the business, you need to think about the 'lifetime value' digital assets and the 'dynamic value' digital assets. Digital assets are unlikely to last more than a lifetime because the digital world is changing so rapidly.

If we look at LinkedIn as an example. The 'lifetime value' of your personal profile is the content that is always visible – your profile details, the posts you write, the list of groups you have joined and the companies you have followed. If you provide an endorsement or a recommendation for someone, this also puts your details on their profile and increases your lifetime value once again.

However, when you Like, Comment or Share an update, it only appears in the newsfeed for a short duration. If you are participating in a closed group, your message is only seen by the people in that group. When you make a new Connection, an announcement may occur but not always.

If you do not participate in any of these 'dynamic' activities, you are unlikely to maximize your digital asset as most digital assets need to be fully completed and active to attract results. What you do need to think about is which activities you will complete for the maximum effect. Not all of them will lead to a direct benefit (if you do this then this happens), but as part of a package, your digital assets can be a very strong business magnet.

Just as you value and depreciate your fixed and current assets, I strongly encourage you to build your digital asset portfolio and review it on a regular basis to make sure it is working effectively. Your number one digital asset is usually your own website – because you can keep this asset indefinitely and it will not be as susceptible to algorithm changes (if you have set it up right and continue to add fresh content). That said, your dynamic activities may be what makes your business go to the next level, especially if your content (pre-selling) goes viral!

Action 59: *Build the fixed, current and digital assets of your business so that you can continue to attract the right type of business and build the asset value of the business. If you do this, when it is time to sell the business, you will receive a good return on your investment of time, money and energy*

8.10 Investment Value In Business

Selling your business is one option after you have been in business for a while – another option is attracting investors! This is particularly important if you wish to consider increasing the scale or size of your business or continue on an innovation path where more funds are needed for research, development or equipment that improves efficiency. You may also wish to acquire other businesses and make them a part of your offering.

Before an investor will consider your business as a viable enterprise, they will do their research. They will want to have details of your performance over time, the market conditions (now and in the future) and the strength of the competition. You may feel that your business is worth a million dollars, they may say $50,000 at best.

If you want to attract investors, you need to find out how valuations are calculated so that when they ask you their questions, you will be able to provide accurate answers. You also need to understand what they want in exchange for their contribution – after all, they will want a good return on their investment, particularly if your offering is classified as speculative.

The better value you offer, the better investor you can attract. The more reliable your data, results and ability to continually perform, the better. You may even be able to attract multiple investors!

What you must do to protect yourself is have a legal representative review any final documentation before you sign it. In my view, you also have to be willing to potentially grow exponentially and work on the business rather than it or potentially lose everything – not everyone can make that type of decision. I can tell you that I have heard plenty of horror stories about business partners and family businesses and Uncle Jack losing his entire retirement fund etc.

Some business owners decide right from the beginning that they want to keep full control of their operations and they only want the business to be a certain size so that they can manage it on their own. This is a perfectly normal and valid choice. However, I would still suggest that they need to think like an investor so that they can focus on doing what is best for them and their business and also prepare it for a future sale. If they do not keep the records that a potential investor would need, it is going to be quite challenging to re-create this data at short notice (in fact some data would possibly not be available and this could seriously reduce the investment value of the business).

Action 60: *Every business owner needs to think like an investor and collect the information that an investor would need to assess the value of your business. This will help you attract an investor or a good sale price in the future*

9. Audience Attraction Techniques

Identifying the audience you would like to attract based on your purpose requires you to think about where that audience will be so that you can reach that audience. As I have said previously, the audience is not everywhere – so you don't have to go everywhere to find your audience.

Coming up with a definition of the right audience can take some time. It may need to include a broader demographic as well as key individuals. It may also need to be particular companies, social enterprises or government officials.

When you create your audience definition, you may like to consider some of the following variables:

- level of education
- age range
- socioeconomic circumstances
- location
- specific areas of interest
- typical habits and behaviors
- personal views and preferences

For example, I like to work with people who are willing to learn and follow up with action. They are usually self-starters and they know that to move on to the next level of their development, they need to take responsibility for their development. They are both male and female. They are usually over the age of 35 and live relatively close to a major city. They have often lived or worked overseas and they are self-reliant and resilient.

This contrasts very differently from one of my clients. She works with people who need personal counselling. These clients need a great deal of support and encouragement to take the next step to improve their future. They want specific instructions and tailored guidance. They may not have a formal education and they are nervous about their next steps. They may have been isolated for some time and they are usually under the age of 40. These people congregate in very different locations to my potential clients.

Alternatively, you could be looking for work and you need to find a suitable employer. Some people prefer working for large organizations, other people prefer to work in small businesses. There is no need to spend time attracting the wrong type of employers, but it is important for you to spend the right amount of time attracting the desired employers. If you can be very clear about the type of employer you would like to work for, you will have a much greater chance of finding this employer. For a start, you won't even consider a job where it is not a good fit.

Finally, you may have a business that sells a range of products. You could be selling those products to customers (B2C) or to businesses (B2B). You may be selling them locally or internationally. You may work closely with other like-minded businesses or be very exclusive. Your purchasers could be looking for a budget price or high-end quality. If you use the right techniques, you are much more likely to attract the right audience.

Essentially, to find the right target audience, you need to define your target audience first. And you need to work out where they congregate so that you can reach them.

Action 61: *Carefully defining your target audience will allow you to calculate where they congregate so that you can select the best methods for attracting them to you for a career or business*

9.1 Identifying Audience Locations

If you have a very clear definition of your target audience, you may already know where they are and how to reach them. For example, I had a course participant who had an interest in 18th Century manuscript writing and he knew the top 20 experts in the world and how to contact them directly – he had decided to create a new website so he could easily share his content with them more frequently.

If you have a broader definition of the type of person you wish to attract, you may choose to start from a place where there is already a large audience that can be segmented. The most obvious example for me of this location is Facebook (at present). They have developed very sophisticated processes to identify individual groups of people and they give you the ability to market directly to these people (for a fee of course!).

If you have a very targeted group of people, say for example, members of the legal profession, you can consider becoming involved with their professional association and attend their events, participate in their online forums or have your articles published in their publications. This will increase your chances of attracting the right career or business in a specific niche.

When considering your various audience locations, consider the:

- reach – general or specific
- size of the audience - large or small
- level of engagement – active or not active
- credibility – high or low
- reliability – professional or personal
- relevance – are they interested in what you have to offer
- interest – do they value what you are offering
- expense – cost to play in that space

I also believe that you should reach slightly beyond your exact target audience. If you can build a general reputation and brand as well as a specific reputation and brand, you are more likely to widen your horizons and gain general attraction as well as specific attraction opportunities. It is interesting to see how many general opportunities have led to very specific opportunities.

For example, I remember interviewing a woman some time ago and she worked with very large corporate organizations helping move senior executives across the world. She simply said to me, if you can convince the right boss's wife, you will get the business. In this case, if she had been exclusively chasing the senior corporate decision maker, she may never have reached them or been able to bypass the gatekeepers!

Ultimately, my best advice, like I suggest for so many aspects of attracting the right career or business, is to utilize a range of multiple concurrent strategies. However, you can be savvy and select the best methods rather than just any methods.

So many people fall into the trap of doing what they think will work – but not utilizing a technique that has been tried and tested. For example, if you come across too forcefully in your approach, you run the risk of gaining a bad reputation. Other people may be reluctant to do anything too different to what they have done in the past and yet they could be missing out on wonderful opportunities.

The goal of this process of identifying your audience location is to reach your target audience, nurture them effectively and then make it easy for them to select you for the career or business opportunity you are offering.

Action 62: *Before choosing the most appropriate target audience locations, test and assess their ability to convince your target audience of your value offering. Make sure that what you do offer is clearly visible to the target audience (without being forceful) so that they can select you for the right career or business opportunity*

9.2 Arousing Your Target Audience

Most people will confirm that they did not secure a job or do business the very first time they met a targeted individual. It can happen though, if the person has gone through a pre-selling approach first.

The pre-selling may have been created by someone else or by you. For example, I am always intrigued when I see an advertisement on television for fresh bananas because obviously the advertisement was not sponsored by every banana grower, but in theory, every banana grower can benefit from the advertisement.

Conversely, you may have gone to great lengths to reach people who are interested in you as a person for a role or your products or services. If they are now ready for the next step, you need to make sure that you arouse them in the right way so that they move towards a decision in your favor.

What has been proven over time is that the more personalized the experience is, the more likely a person is to agree to a career or business opportunity or engage with what is on offer. If their journey up to this point has been a good and comprehensive experience, the final decision is much more likely to be successful. In a career, this usually means that the person will perform well in the job and stay with the enterprise – in business, it means that the customer will consider additional purchases in the future.

This pre-purchase journey can be improved significantly if:

- the process is quick (speed is becoming a key factor in most exchanges – even in recruitment)
- the person is treated respectfully and is not forced or rushed into a decision at any point
- an adequate amount of reliable information is automatically available for review and verification
- the person's expectations are met or exceeded
- it is easy for the person to make a final decision and carry out the transaction
- there is a guarantee or a safety net available if absolutely necessary

I believe that it is fair to say that most people do not expect a 'free lunch' but they do expect a 'good lunch.' If you have identified someone as a prospect and you arouse their interest effectively, you have a much greater chance of attracting the right career or business.

Action 63: *Helping your target audience understand what you have to offer as a career or business in a timely, effective and informative way will significantly increase your ability to attract the right career or business*

9.3 Discouraging Your Non Target Audience

If you have started attracting the wrong type of interest from the wrong employers or customers, it is time to adjust your target audience attraction techniques.

In the past, when instant messaging first became available, I would find all sorts of people wanting to text chat with me during my working day. It is not that I didn't want to help people, I simply could not afford the time to sit and type countless messages with people who had no intention of doing business with me. More recently, I started receiving LinkedIn messages from people who wanted me to assist them free of charge.

I have also heard of people who have wasted hours of their time answering telephone calls, responding to lengthy emails or posts on social media and preparing extensive proposals that do not lead to paying work.

Most small businesses simply do not have the time to spend on these people that I sometimes refer to as 'tire kickers.' This is an expression from the car sales industry. People who come in and look at a car and kick the tires but have no intention of ever purchasing a car.

I also want to state up front that I do not have any hesitation in sharing what I know. I am more than willing at any time to pass on the best and most useful information to whoever asks me a question. I simply do not have the time to provide all of that personalized assistance for free to everyone.

So, to overcome this issue, I publish an enormous amount of free information online. If the person is genuinely in a position of disadvantage, they can access all of these resources at no cost. In fact they may be able to find everything they need without paying me one cent.

However, if they want my personal advice for their personal situation, I have decided that there needs to be some form of value exchange. So to prevent a huge onslaught of email questions, I make it very clear that free information is available and I direct people to that information (and when they do contact me directly, I give them direct links). I also make it clear that if they would like personal assistance, there is a fee. The genuine people then come back to me and book an appointment. The other people usually never contact me again.

I feel good because I know that the information I have provided will be helpful to them and I have not wasted hours of my time with a person who is not part of my target audience. The people who do not pay for any information may still recognize the value of the free information and recommend me in the future to someone else.

I also readily provide my contact details so that if the person is prepared to pay, they can easily make an appointment. Likewise, with my 120 Ways Publishing website, if the person wants to purchase a digital copy of one of my books, they can do so directly and I don't need to personally manage that process.

The style of my online and offline message also affects the type of people I attract. So again, if you find that you are attracting the wrong type of interest, ask yourself, are you creating the right image?

This is particularly important in relation to your career. If you are wanting a promotion, are you acting and dressing as someone who would be suitable for the next level role? Are you proactive in your approach or are you just sitting and waiting and hoping? I remember very early in my career arriving at work with wet hair because I didn't allow enough time in the morning to get ready for work – that hardly made me promotion worthy at the time! I soon changed my ways.

If you are in business, are you keeping up to date with the most effective trends and improvements? Are you upgrading your processes on an incremental basis so that you are not suddenly faced with a huge expense if a key component of your enterprise becomes obsolete?

When you first start working, you may not necessarily try and find the absolute best job from day one – you may be happy with a job that is 'okay for now.' When a business first starts out, they often accept business from customers or clients outside of their ideal target audience to keep the cash flow going. However, you will find that most businesses start to do very well when they start saying 'no' to the clients or customers that are not ideal. They may even recommend someone else or as I have done, provide alternative information for free.

The point I am trying to make is rather than assuming that attracting the right career or business is all about increasing the size of your target audience, sometimes it is about decreasing the size of your target audience but qualifying that target audience before you do business. This can save you a great deal of wasted time, chasing invoice payments because they are reluctant purchasers and overall stress when they argue about the value you are offering. An ideal target client will happily pay because they understand that what you have to offer matches their needs.

Action 64: *Having the courage to qualify your target audience or say no if they ask for something outside of your value offering has the potential to help you attract the right career or business as well as save you the time, energy and stress of the wrong opportunity*

9.4 Re-Attracting Your Target Audience

We all know that most living creatures respond to positive reinforcement. If good behavior is rewarded, it is likely to be repeated.

I ordered some printer ink from a local supplier and when it arrived, there were two wrapped chocolates in the box. Now there is absolutely no logical reason for the ink supplier to add chocolates to my order as it will not make the printer ink last longer or perform better in my printer, but for me as the customer, I received a very nice surprise – I was rewarded for making a purchase.

Not every customer will want to receive chocolate with their order, but I can assure you, I have re-ordered ink multiple times thanks to those first two chocolates. What I don't like are those annoying 'please complete a review' forms that keep me answering 20 questions after I have stayed in a hotel room for one night!

So when thinking about your target audience, the ones that have already provided you with a career or business opportunity, think about what will attract them back to you in the future. How will you maintain your relationship with them? Will it be an active pursuit or a passive pursuit? Will they just 'see' you appear in their social media news feed or will they receive something directly from you?

After all of the time and effort you have put in to attracting them to you, it is much easier to keep them associated with you than start with a brand new person over and over again. Even if this individual does not assist you directly again, they can be a referral source, so technically, they are still part of your target audience. If they become a referral point for multiple opportunities, even better.

Basic marketing will always teach you that it is usually much easier to sell a new product to an existing customer than a new product to a new customer. Keep this in mind when selecting audience attraction techniques.

Action 65: *Re-attracting your existing target audience can be far more effective than starting with a new target audience for each and every career or business opportunity*

10. Content Attraction Techniques

I have been publishing online content since 2001 when my first website Newcomers Network http://newcomersnetwork.com went online. In the early days, it was quite easy for my website to attract 60,000 unique visits a month because there were not as many websites and most websites did not have very much information on them (they were mostly brochure style websites).

Now, there is so much user-generated content it is hard to even comprehend how much information is available online. Newspaper journalists who would previously generate one or two articles per day are now competing with online news portals sharing one or two articles per journalist per hour.

If you are someone who likes to write, make audio or video recordings or produce some form of content either online or offline, you can definitely use content to attract a career or business opportunity.

If you are someone who does not like to produce content, you have some other alternatives. You can:

- curate other people's content by compiling a list of relevant information
- share other people's content in relevant forums and gain credibility for recognizing the quality of that information
- outsource your content creation by working with a ghost writer or paying someone to produce content that you have commissioned and will appear under your name
- interact with other people's content – like, comment or share information as it appears so that you can be perceived as informed and current and willing to interact

You can also consider various content locations – not just online. Magazines that have managed to survive in an online world have obviously managed to create content that people are willing to pay for. In-house publications, journals, books and local newspapers can also be helpful. There are a huge range of podcasts, vodcasts, videos, radio stations, television stations (free to air and paid or cable), billboards, bus shelters, shop windows, noticeboards, apps and more.

Significant media publicity also has the potential to generate a huge audience in an instant. Preparing the right content for that opportunity is vital. However, you need to have your information ready at a moment's notice.

Before selecting the content that you will share (either your own or someone else's), remember that if you are trying to attract the best career or business opportunity, you should be aiming to share the best content not just bulk content.

Action 66: *There are many places where you can publish your own content or share content that you have curated, found, outsourced or interacted with. Sharing this content in the best locations for your target audience is a key to attracting the right career or business opportunity*

10.1 Content Guidelines

As you already know, there is a huge amount of content out there in the world. However, if you read something, it does not make you a qualified expert – that usually requires a combination of information, practice, mistakes, corrections, experience, review and feedback. As the saying goes, text does not give context.

You may also feel partly intimidated by either publishing your own story (in your resume, CV, LinkedIn Profile, website or blog) or your business story. You may think that there is 'no point' stating the bleeding obvious. Unfortunately if you don't tell, you can't sell.

Did you know that you do not necessarily need to provide unique content? You simply have to provide quality content. Be clear about what you say and how you say it. I have a policy of not criticizing anyone and always providing solutions.

Content that is evergreen (current today, tomorrow, next week) has a longer lifetime value – so I do encourage you consider spending most of your time sharing evergreen content. However, just as we have discussed lifetime value and dynamic value in this book, there is also value in evergreen content and current or real time content.

If you create the right message with your content, you are much more likely to generate engagement. Content has also been recognized as one of the best ways to nurture a relationship.

I have discovered that people really respond to content that:

- feels real, genuine, authentic and truthful
- is concise and conversational but still with some depth (no waffle – only information that is contextually relevant)
- tells a story (preferably a human story rather than a brand story)
- is original
- is balanced and insightful
- educates the reader and answers multiple questions
- is what the audience or consumers want
- explains how to do something
- solves a problem or suggests solutions
- provides value
- is a bit raw and personal
- uses emotional or hypnotic language
- is entertaining, engaging and fun
- is believable and verifiable and includes stats and facts
- exceeds expectations by providing value and relevancy
- is credible and has a certain level of authority
- has a catchy headline and a great first sentence
- also includes a video
- encourages comments and asks questions
- is accurate (no spelling or grammar mistakes)
- has been proof read and edited so that it reads well
- is easily readable on a mobile device
- is consistent with your main message and reinforces your main message

Here are some ideas for headline formulas or article content:

- how to
- ask a question
- list of (sometimes called a listicle)
- number of
- opinion piece
- commentary piece
- analysis of a situation
- special insight or breaking story
- alignment with a current event or calendar date
- prestigious award announcement
- case study relevant to the target audience
- tutorial on a particular topic or skill
- quotes or motivational or inspirational messages

If you are still stuck for ideas, consider looking at what other influencers, thought leaders and experts are publishing and consider how your content may align or complement their offering.

There are many reasons why people are attracted to good content. In most cases, it gives people knowledge and a sense of power from having that knowledge. These people understand that ignorance can be costly and even lead to unnecessary expense.

If you are new to writing, you may like to consider just writing for yourself first – just so that you can get into the habit of condensing your ideas and distilling your thoughts. You could also ask a trusted advisor to give you their thoughts before you publish your content.

There is an expression I really like by Jonathan Swift. "Words are the clothing of our thoughts." Writing gives me the ability to process my thoughts and share my ideas in a more concise way. If I tried to act out what I believed, that could take years!!! It is also a little harder to distribute!

If you decide to publish content online, make sure that you have registered your website or blog with http://archive.org/web/ so that it remains on the internet archive for people to view in the future.

Action 67: *There are some general principles for creating good quality evergreen and current content that will help you attract the right career or business and nourish your relationships. Be courageous and ready to share your story so that you can be found*

10.2 Content Conversions

There is not a lot of point in producing quality content if it doesn't lead to conversions – and that means either the right career or business opportunity for you. Try not to judge your content by what you have said, judge it by the response you receive.

Some people seek 'vanity metrics' – loads of views or likes – but if it doesn't lead to the career or business opportunity you are seeking, what is the point?

There are some essential ingredients you need to consider to make sure that your content does convert:

- it needs to include a call to action or offer
- it needs to have a distinct focus and purpose
- be easily found if someone is looking for that information (preferably on the first page of internet search results)
- it needs to include the most important attributes (keywords, details, solution)
- it needs to reach the right people
- it needs to lead towards a resolution or solve a problem
- it needs to show how someone can be helped (rather than tell them what to do)
- it needs to include good quality visual images (if that option is available)
- it needs to be verifiable with either relevant facts, social proof or reviews
- it needs to not just sell but lead to 'devotion' and an ongoing interest in you or your business

- it needs to lead to referrals
- it needs to be easy to scan (so people can 'read' it by just skimming over the headlines)
- it needs to be easy to share and shareable (people want to share it)
- it can be co-created to drive higher engagement and reach
- if it is for business purposes, it needs to answer the top three objections, explain how the product or service solves the customers need and how your product or service is unique

If you have paid any sort of fee to have your content published (either because it is on a fee for service website or it is part of an advertisement or advertorial), it is particularly important that you make sure your content includes your keywords and your key messages, a link to your landing page or website, relevant images or videos to create extra visual impact and a call to action.

If you are sharing your content on social media, make sure you use the relevant hash tags (if appropriate) or personal handles (like @sueellson or @120ways).

If you are only creating content that could be classified as 'click bait' – the best you can expect is a few sales. You are more likely to receive 'click conversions' if you can demonstrate value. Whatever you do, it is a good idea to have a look at the data you can collect and then test and measure what is actually happening so that you can increase the time you spend on what works and decrease the time you spend on what doesn't work.

Action 68: *Content is an excellent tool for attracting opportunities for your career or business but it needs to convert to be of real benefit. Make sure you include the essential ingredients so that your content does convert*

10.3 Content Reach

If your content reaches just one person and that leads to the exact career or business opportunity that you want – congratulations! However, the likelihood of this happening increases if more if the right people see your content.

Most people, as already mentioned, seek vanity results – lots of likes or high circulation numbers or thousands of viewers. What provides even more significant value is if one person doesn't take just one action (for example a Like), if each person who sees the content completes another viral action (for example a Share or tells their friend at work). A Share is much more valuable because it sends the content to another network which can then allow the content to be shared with another network and then another network and so on.

Online content shared on various websites and platforms is also measured in different ways:

- how long the viewer spends reading the content
- how many headings and links are included
- how many labelled images or videos are included
- how quickly the author responds to any comments or feedback
- how many different sources lead to the content (and the quality of those sources)
- how many people like, comment on or share the content
- how long the content remains relevant
- whether or not the content is updated
- how long ago the content was published
- how well the article performs in search results etc

The important point I would like to make is that what works today in terms of content performance may not work tomorrow. Some platforms, when publishing was initially encouraged, shared newly published content to most of the people connected to the person publishing the content.

Nowadays, the content distribution algorithms have changed significantly and although you may be connected to thousands of people, as little as 2% of those people may be notified about your content (unless you pay an extra fee). However, if people regularly interact with your content, this percentage can increase without a payment.

If you really want your content to go viral, firstly, it should be extremely good quality and secondly, you might like to trigger some of that viral activity to get the ball rolling. If you can develop a good relationship with other people who are willing to like, comment or share your content, fantastic. You may work on a 'tag exchange' basis – you tag them on your articles so your item appears in their news feed and they tag you on their articles so their item appears in your news feed. You need to have a certain level of trust to implement this process.

There are also several automation tools. For example, if you add a new post to your WordPress Website, it can automatically share the details on Twitter, Facebook etc.

The essential idea here is that your content collects people, connects them to you in some way and then you convert them in a way that helps you achieve your purpose. We talked earlier in the book about building your digital assets and content is a great way to do this – you can essentially create a content bank. The more deposits you make, the better!

There are many content marketers providing tips and tricks on how to make content marketing work for you. They will try and help you automate your content distribution – however, it is still important for you to manually respond to any conversation that is created (I have been the recipient of templated responses and I hate it! The publisher instantly loses all credibility).

You may have noticed that platforms like Facebook don't create any of their content – their users do – and their users share it all too! They have developed a business that allows for automatic scalability, virtually zero cost of production, is profitable and the only time they spend is making sure that the system works and can easily handle advertising requests! No wonder it is such a profitable platform.

The final comment I will make in relation to content reach is your personal requirement to align the content reach with a particular geographic location. If you really want to attract a career or business in the local area, you need to make sure that your content is published in local resources. If these websites are 'high authority' websites (like local government, suburb directories, major enterprises or publications), then your content will perform particularly well in search results in that location – by either people on their phone in the location or people adding the location name to their search query.

Action 69: *Utilize various techniques to help your content reach your target audience through viral processes. Try to design your content and your sharing strategies so that they automatically trigger these processes without payment*

10.4 Content Sharing

Once you start creating content, particularly online content, you may be very tempted to re-purpose your content and share the same article in multiple locations. Unfortunately, this is not a good search engine optimization strategy as search engines want to give searchers the best search result for their query. They don't want to give 10 identical results and if there are 10 identical results, you risk having your content removed from the search index.

To overcome this challenge, I suggest that you choose where you would like to publish your content first. If you are wanting to target airline travelers, have it published in the airline magazine – but afterwards (at least one week after publication), if you have the publisher's permission, reproduce the content on your own website as an 'archive' version. If they do not want you to re-produce the content, you can still mention what you had published and where on your own website (and/or list it on your LinkedIn Profile under Publications).

When you archive your content, add some additional information – like a link to the original piece, the location of the publication, date, who commissioned the piece, provide a digital image of the original piece (re-sized so that it loads quickly on a mobile device), the authors, the word count etc – this way, the second version of the article will be slightly different to the first version and it has a chance to also appear on the first page of search engine results – but more importantly, if the original publisher removes the content from their publication, an archive version remains in your possession.

If you forgot to do this at the time of the original publication, you may like to visit the http://archive.org website and see if the original version has been indexed.

So, as a priority, make sure you share your content on your own website. The next place to consider sharing your content is through other broadcast channels - your own email newsletter, social media, online forums etc. However, when you share it in these locations, please be mindful of the relevant etiquette for each channel. If sharing a link doesn't create a picture on the screen, see if you can add an image before posting. Make sure you include hash tags (#subjects of your content) and acknowledge the publisher (@publisher). Don't just link to your archive version on your website, do the right thing and link to the original version on the first publisher's website.

The next place to share your content is through people you know – other friends, colleagues, staff members, affiliates, alliance partners etc. You can do this by 'tagging' them (as mentioned previously) or by contacting them directly and encouraging them to do this for you. If they are willing to share your content, please make sure you acknowledge their efforts (with a Like and a Comment if available) and make an effort to personally thank them directly (and publicly if appropriate).

Algorithms may like it when someone Likes or Comments but they love it when someone Shares content – so the aim in all of these cases is to encourage people to share content (but please remember the first principle, it needs to be good quality content, not just a sales pitch).

Another place to share your content is by direct message to targeted individuals. If you know your network well, you may be aware of one or more people who would really like to read some content you have found or produced so you could approach them directly and send through the details. They may be so appreciative that they then forward it on again.

You may also like to gently encourage them when you send them a message. For example, "Hi Jane and Nick, I had an article on the topic of 'How to choose your next job or career' published at http://www.linkedin.com/pulse/how-choose-your-next-job-career-sue-ellson and thought it may be of interest to you or someone you know. Please feel free to share it around your networks and let me know if you have any questions. Cheers, Sue Ellson."

These processes may appear to be quite time consuming when you complete them for the first time. Let me assure you, they become very quick and easy once you have done it a few times. I am encouraging you to follow this process because producing content is not always a five minute task. It usually requires quite a bit of thought time, even if you write quickly. You also need to secure the writing opportunity in the first place. It is very tempting, after going through all this to fall in a heap, exhausted and grateful – but if you really want to maximize your attraction power, you need to increase the size of your 'spider's web.' It is a lot easier to use one piece of content in at least two or more ways than reinvent the wheel for every single piece of content and miss out on the lifetime value of keeping an archive version on your own website.

Action 70: *Content that you write or help produce needs to be recorded, archived and shared to gain maximum attraction power. To secure lifetime value, add the details to your own website and to secure dynamic value, share it through other broadcast channels and individuals*

10.5 Content Critics

I have found that the people most critical of any content written are the people who actually wrote the content – in other words, you if you have written it! Some people are so paralyzed by how people may interpret their writing that they refuse to publish any content. Other people have been criticized in their early years and have lost all confidence in writing.

Before I wrote my first book, I made the general assumption that I could write adequately because I had written a lot of articles and I had received mostly positive feedback. What I have found interesting is that the more I write (80,000 words in the first book, over 40,000 words in this book so far), the more my writing has improved.

When I look back on my earlier pieces, I can see how they could be improved, but I remind myself that they were based on my skills at that time. I was also given an extra boost of confidence when my professional author adviser told me that I write very well. Remember to listen to praise, not just criticism.

Please do not keep your internal voice silent because of fear. There will always be some people who like what you have to say and other people who are not interested in what you have to say. I don't expect everyone to read what I have written. What I do appreciate is the ability to share what I have learnt so that others can benefit from my experience.

Julián Martínez Nicolás says that "Reading makes you free, writing makes you eternal." I encourage you to be brave and share your story so that you can attract the right career or business. If your story is not shared and available, how do you expect to be found? Who will miss a fabulous opportunity because you were too scared to share your wisdom? Be bold, be brave – you are important!

There are other people who may also be critical of your writing or content. People you know who feel threatened by your success or intimidated because they do not have the confidence to write. There may also be people who genuinely do not like your writing for a valid reason (it may not be backed up by evidence, it has spelling and grammar mistakes etc).

I manage my own personal reaction to criticism by looking very closely at my intention when I am writing. My main goal is to write 'solution-focused' content. I am always aiming to educate, inform and entertain my readers. My ultimate goal is for the reader to interpret the information for their needs and take action that will help them move closer to their values and purpose.

That means that whenever I receive any form of criticism, I look at that criticism very closely. I try and understand the reason behind the criticism. I never retaliate with further criticism. I always acknowledge the person's concern, I always apologize if any offence has occurred (even if it is not my fault) and I always encourage further clarification and ramification, even if it is at my own expense.

A typical example of criticism is a bad review. Many businesses worry about bad reviews. I accept bad reviews as a way to improve my offering – to 'sharpen the saw.' I make every effort to respond as quickly as possible. I provide an appropriate response publicly and I also attempt to contact the person directly for a specific resolution. I do not wish to entertain a public battle. I also thank them for their feedback and their willingness to come forward and raise their concerns.

By being very clear on my intention and willing to discuss any concerns politely, I have actually managed to learn and grow from every confrontation. During the disagreement, I do feel personally challenged – even if I am not at fault. I have learnt to accept that sometimes it is absolutely not my fault, it is simply a perception that was incorrectly created. However, for the other person, it was real – so I do my best to help both of us come to an appropriate understanding.

Challenges are a great way to help us grow and develop. Can you imagine moving to the next level of your development by sitting on a beach under a nice palm tree? If you were meditating, I believe you could – but for most of us, we need to be pushed outside of our comfort zone to move forward. I have had to develop a 'thick skin' and learn to be more resilient. To not take things so personally (even though I still do). If I get too down in the dumps about a particular situation, I call for back up. I go and see someone I know who does believe in me – so don't be afraid to reach out for a comforting hand if you need one. Just because one person is difficult it doesn't mean that everyone is difficult!

Action 71: *Overcoming your own internal critical voice or someone else's criticism is not always easy but several strategies can be used to help you grow and develop from the experience*

11. People Attraction Techniques

For centuries, humans have lived as tribes. We have discovered that there is safety in numbers. Most of us also know that we can probably run fast if we do things on our own, but we can run a lot further if we have a team travelling with us.

The most successful individuals and businesses do not work in isolation – they work in partnership with others – either regularly or as required – but they rarely work completely alone.

It is my personal belief that we are biologically programmed to be social creatures – to need the company of other human beings. I believe that this is true for extroverts (who gain their energy from being with other people) as well as for introverts (who gain their energy from within).

An introvert may need to spend most of their time on their own and this doesn't make them weird. However, they still need to go about their daily routine and they will need to interact with other people. They will find it extremely important to find the right people to help them attract the right career or business because the wrong person is likely to annoy them immensely! An extrovert may be able to tolerate someone who is not quite the right fit because they still gain energy from them.

There are also introverts, like me, who like people and enjoy their company, but don't gain their energy from being with other people. I like teaching and helping lots of people, but at the end of the day, I am very comfortable retreating to my cave and having time to myself. Did you know that many actors are also introverts?

Before you start to think about what sorts of people you want to attract into your life for your career or business (sorry, I am not here to help you attract a life partner!), you need to think about the types of people that would be most helpful.

Consider some of the following variables:

- their values and beliefs (if there is a clash, this is problematic)
- their physical proximity

- their education level
- their socioeconomic status and income
- their personality type
- their ability to empathize with you and understand you
- their availability and cost
- their level of influence
- their willingness to help you or partner with you
- their hobbies and interests
- their attitude and ability to communicate
- the way that they challenge and inspire you
- the level of trust you have developed

My Accountability Partner passes all of my selection criteria.

You may find that some variables could be ranked slightly higher than others, but for the most important variables, you need to be aligned (at average or above). You may find that some variables are essential (like trust) and other variables less important (like hobbies and interests).

If you want to attract the right types of people into your life for your career or business, you need to think very carefully about your criteria. You may also need several different people as it is unusual to find all of the qualities in one person.

Let's look at an example. You have a best friend that you have known since school. You have always been able to spend time together and have fun. However, more recently, you have been thinking about pursuing your passion for art. Your friend suggests that you are a little crazy – why would you want to give up a successful career and a reliable pay packet to pursue art? How will you pay for your children's education? This person may be a wonderful friend, but will they help you attract the right career or business in the future? Are they able to encourage you or help you or will they only criticize you?

I am not suggesting that you should stop seeing your school friend. What I am suggesting is that if you really did want to follow your passion for art, you would need to attract some new people into your life who could help you on that part of your journey. I am also not suggesting that you quit your job today and start art classes tomorrow. I believe that a successful transition involves gradual steps and a clever strategy rather than a knee jerk reaction.

Action 72: *To attract the right career or business opportunity, you need to think about what sort of people could help you on your journey. You also need to establish some selection criteria so that you can adopt a more targeted approach when sourcing these people*

11.1 People Background Research

Now that you have come up with a definition of the type of people who can help you on your journey, you need to learn more about the people who might be suitable. A good place to start is with the Thought Leaders or Experts in your profession or industry.

By investigating the stories behind these people, you will start to find out how they achieved success. They will usually reveal, in some public manner, the secrets to their success. They will give you clues like:

- they had an inspirational teacher or lecturer at school or university
- their parents always encouraged them
- they worked with multiple mentors or coaches
- they sought specific professional advice
- they trusted their gut (but always kept an eye out for opportunities)
- they developed certain personal skills (decision making, resilience etc)
- they always knew in their heart that it was what they wanted to do
- they persisted despite multiple challenges
- they relied on other people
- they got a fantastic 'break' and were in the right place at the right time

- they went away for a period of time to evaluate all of their options
- they tried and failed until something worked
- they kept going despite making mistakes or losing everything along the way

When you understand their stories and their backgrounds, you will start to gain clues as to the specific qualities of the people you would like to attract into your life. You will start to identify with their challenges and develop some confidence because you have probably overcome similar challenges. You will also gain a clearer picture of where you would like to be in the future.

You will start to visualize what is possible. You will be able to create a new picture with your flavor. You will understand that it takes commitment, responsibility and persistence – but it is achievable.

Many years ago I heard two expressions that have remained with me ever since. The first one was that there is no such thing as a new idea. I was devastated! I really did believe I had come up with several great ideas. So I thought about it a little more and I realized that every idea is partly based on another idea – but it can be a new variation!

The second expression was that it takes 20 years to be an overnight success. This is probably true if you do not take the steps you need to take in years 1, 2, 3, 4 etc. If you dogmatically follow your ideas without reviewing what actually works, it literally could take you 20 years to try and test all of the variables. So rather than reinvent the wheel, gain some inside knowledge by looking at what other people have done in your niche and borrow the tried and tested ideas that will work for you.

For example, in my case, I have completed a lot of personal development courses and read a lot of books and articles around my areas of interest. I don't need more people telling me what to do, what I need is encouragement and support to keep doing it (like most people, I have procrastinated in the past)! So most of the people in my inner circle are the types of people who do encourage me to keep taking action. I have now moved to another level and am going to work with a professional coach who can recommend more effective strategies than the ones I am currently using – and he has already passed my key selection criteria.

Action 73: *Do some background research on the key people in your career or business field that have been successful and find out what their 'secrets to success' have been. This will help you determine the types of people you need to find to assist you on your journey*

11.2 Finding The Right People

When you have a clear definition of the people you would like to meet, you have a much better chance of finding them. I would like to share some interesting sources:

- university lecturers and tutors
- fellow students in a course you are studying (or have studied in the past)
- social occasions when you are casually chatting
- interest groups, sports or hobbies (just let people know about your interests)
- cold calling or emailing people you have found through research and asking for information or a referral
- attending events
- finding out where they go and going there (specific events, fairs, conferences, groups)
- via voluntary work or a lower level role in a target enterprise
- through a mentor that you may have found or been referred to (you may be able to find their contact details via https://rocketreach.co)
- recruiters, head hunters, human resource managers or outplacement specialists
- freelancer listings (especially if they have earned excellent reviews or multiple assignments)
- asking around your local community or doing research internationally
- identifying someone who is doing something similar in another non-competing location
- through an internship, apprenticeship or work placement

- talking to people you meet on public transport or whilst walking your dog or someone else's dog
- profile pages on websites for businesses, people, industries, associations
- major publications – contact some bloggers, journalists or editors for a referral
- by asking everyone you meet

There are no limitations on where you can meet people – either online or in person. One of my clients found me when she met a guy from a dating website and he referred her to me. I have heard of many long term business relationships that were started after a long haul aircraft flight. You could even ask around your family and friends circle – you are unlikely to know everyone they already know.

Whilst there are many places to find people, if you are time poor, it is a good idea to concentrate on the places where you are most likely to find the specific people you are seeking.

To be attractive to people, you must be able to smile. It is a universal greeting of friendship and it encourages good conversation. If you have a serious face all the time, you will not appear attractive – even if you are beautiful or handsome.

If you are constantly thinking about what must be done and how it must be completed, you will not necessarily be open to new opportunities. If you are crystal clear about the types of people you would like to meet, provided you take some action in that direction, it is amazing how often these people will simply appear as if completely out of the blue. Remember to follow up with all of them, even if they are not a 'perfect' fit and treat every person respectfully, even if they do not meet your career or business selection criteria. Say thank you whenever possible.

Action 74: *Put on a smile and get out and about both online and offline to meet people that can help you on your journey to attracting the right career or business*

11.3 Building The Relationship

Trust is most commonly earned over time, it is not something that automatically happens. If you are out and about networking or producing content online, you cannot expect that the first time you connect with someone, they will want to hire you or do business with you.

In online business, there is a suggestion that on average, a potential customer will consume 11 hours of content, connect or correspond seven times and need to see you on four different channels (personally, in a group, on a website, on social media etc) before they will make a buying decision.

It is possible for someone to simply walk into a shop and buy a product, but why did they choose that shop in the first place? Will they be pleased if you greet them and ask them if they are happy browsing or would they prefer to be left alone?

If you have found someone that you would like to reach out to, there is a lot of background research that you can do beforehand. It is prudent for you to at least do a preliminary internet search and a more in depth search by looking at the various links associated with that person's name and/or keywords and/or company name.

You may also like to have a closer look on their individual profiles on LinkedIn, Facebook etc and their own website. You can also utilize a social media or people aggregator browser extension or fee for service program – like http://connectifier.com (acquired by LinkedIn) or https://www.crystalknows.com

Some of these services offer computer generated insights into a person's personality (https://www.crystalknows.com). This may or may not be entirely accurate, but I always find it interesting!

Gaining this background information gives you an opportunity to make a more meaningful connection with a targeted individual.

I encourage you to make the initial contact by telephone if possible because they can hear the sound of your voice and you can have a conversation immediately.

You can start by introducing yourself and explaining how you found their details (the best way is via a referral from someone they already know) and mentioning that you would simply like to ask a few short questions about your future career or business.

The next part of the conversation should be to confirm that now is a suitable time to chat for a few minutes. If it is not, then you can simply ask when would be a convenient time to call back for a few minutes and then return the call at the allocated time.

You can then start asking your pre-prepared information gathering questions. You can wrap up with a sincere thank you and also ask, given the nature of your questions, if there is anything else that they think you should know.

If you would like to establish an ongoing discussion, you might like to ask if it is okay to call them again for any additional questions in the future or you could ask if it would be possible to meet them in person at an event or nearby venue in the coming weeks. You may also like to discuss the possibility of a mentoring relationship – which would involve at least one in person meeting, a weekly phone call and an email here and there for the next three months. You must also ask if a fee would be required. The worst that can happen is they can say 'no.' The best that can happen is they say 'yes' and you have a new mentor!

Starting a relationship, regardless of where it begins, is easy. Maintaining it can take more effort. As a minimum, you need to add the person to your database (or connect with them on LinkedIn) – this way, they will be able to easily find you and be automatically reminded that you exist when your activity is shared.

Significant people really need to be contacted at least three times a year. This will maintain your relationship. It doesn't need to be an hour long meeting each time, but you do need to find ways to automate and also personalize your relationship. You can automate part of the relationship by scheduling a recurring follow up, adding them to a mailing list, attending a regular event that they also attend etc.

At some point, you may also choose not to keep in regular contact. I agree with the expression that people will often come into our life for a reason, a season or a lifetime. I have had good quality relationships with a variety of coaches, mentors and advisers but each one of them has eventually reached a conclusion. If I had not been willing to let go and move on, I am certain that I would not have grown and developed as quickly.

If you feel as if you have plateaued in your life, have a look around and reflect on how much these people challenge and encourage you to grow. They do not need to be abandoned, but if you find an additional person who has already reached the next level and you invite them into your life, you may find yourself moving up to the next level too.

Action 75: *After finding the people who can help you move to the next level, reach out to them, preferably by telephone and ask them questions to find the information you need. If you would like to maintain the relationship, find ways to keep in touch at least three times a year and automate and personalize the process*

11.4 Refining Your People Attraction Techniques

Once you start attracting people into your life that help you move towards your career or business goals, you will suddenly start noticing that even more of these people start appearing.

In a career, it will appear as either managers or other employers who start reaching out to you for a new opportunity. In business, it will be potential clients or customers who want to do business with you.

This is a critical stage. You may be fearful and say no to every opportunity. You may be gung ho and say yes to the first opportunity that comes along (and regret it later). Or you may carefully evaluate what is on offer and make sure it aligns with your values and purpose.

This is when you need to be able to make good quality decisions. You need to be able to sort between the personal, emotional and rational aspects of the opportunity in front of you. You need to be prepared to say 'no' or 'yes' as the case may be. Some people say 'yes' too easily and become overwhelmed. Some people say 'no' and miss good opportunities. Some people don't make any decision at all and wonder why they remain stuck.

If you would like to consider all of your options before you make a decision, tell the person that you need some time to make a decision and agree on a time when you will deliver that decision (and make sure you do). It may also be necessary for the person to make the offer in writing so that you can have some level of confidence that the offer is genuine. If you are still uncertain, you may like to agree to transitional terms rather than final terms.

If you find that connecting with people is fun and exciting, you may be tempted to treat the process as a bit of a sport and a game to be won at all costs. You can actually waste a lot of time and effort if you fall into this trap of just adding more people to your network. You may also find that you end up building your network in the wrong direction and the people you are adding are not related to your original purpose at all.

A very wise business mentor once asked me – "How many hours per day are you spending on billable work and how many hours a day are you spending on attracting work?" The same applies to your career. How much time are you spending on developing the additional skills, knowledge and networks you need for your next role and how much time are you wasting by maintaining the status quo?

An important aspect of attracting the right people into your life involves paying it forward. Yes, you can ask for information, but in return, you should always see if there is something you can offer in exchange. As a minimum, you must always say thank you for any form of assistance you receive.

You may even like to offer something up front with no expectation of an immediate return (I provide a lot of pro-bono presentations for community groups). If you are clear on the types of people you want to attract for your career or business, you can then focus on creating engagement with these people, building and nurturing your network and developing trusted relationships. Trust is gained by observing consistent behavior – it cannot be bought. If it is lost, it can take a long time to recover.

Action 76: *As your personal network grows and opportunities appear, you need to be able to review each career or business opportunity objectively and make good quality decisions. Ultimately, you will need to align your decisions with your values and purpose. Ideally, you will also build trusted relationships along the way*

12. Platform Attraction Techniques

There are so many platforms where you can share your story nowadays that it is almost becoming overwhelming. I will always believe that the highest priority platform should be the one that you can control yourself – that is either you as a person in real life (your behavior and actions) or you virtually (most commonly, your own website or mobile presence).

I encourage every person to register their own domain name (mine is http://sueellson.com). If you have young children, I also encourage you to register a domain name for them too so that they have a better chance of securing a good domain name. If an exact name domain name match is not available, you may like to incorporate a dash, another letter or numbers, a country code, a different extension etc.

I will discuss various additional tips about creating your own website in Section 18.

Before you select which platforms for creating an online profile, please consider the following variables:

- your values and purpose
- the age, quality and reliability of the platform
- the alignment of the audience (overall size or niche size)
- the reach of the platform (is the content exclusive within the platform or publicly searchable)
- the level of user generated or moderator generated activity in the platform (if no-one participates, it could be useless to you)
- the reputation of the platform with your target audience and perhaps the general public
- the safety and security of your information and activity
- the lifetime and dynamic value of your content and activity
- the potential for growth and development in the future (do they have a history of improving the platform?)
- the ability to download an archive of your content and activity (or make an effort to record this separately on your own website or store it in your archive files)

- how much time and effort is involved in maintaining your presence on the platform

Personally, I am more than happy to look at new platforms, but when I do, I only put my toe in the water, not my whole body. I like to have a good look around and do a risk assessment. I like to see how far my message will spread and who will see that message. How likely it is for my content to go viral with my target audience. Ultimately, I want the platform to attract the right opportunities and I want it to do this efficiently and effectively. I also have to add each new platform to my list of usernames and passwords. Periodically, I also go back in and close irrelevant platform accounts. I also have to work out how much time and effort it will take to maintain my involvement – will there be a reasonable return on my investment?

Action 77: *Carefully assess the types of platforms that you can use for your values and purpose. Consider all of the variables before joining and make a reasonable effort to maintain your presence after joining. Be willing to close your account if it no longer serves your purpose*

12.1 Completing Your Platform Profile

There are some traps that you might easily fall into when completing an online profile. If you are not careful, you will automatically give the platform direct access to all of your emails, all of your contacts, all of your internet history and who knows what else! That is why it is extremely important when you sign up for a new account that you very carefully read what is on the screen. They will be sneaky and make their preferred choice very obvious (like a nice big blue button) and your preferred choice simply text on the screen. All I can say is – buyer beware – caveat emptor!

If you are clear on your values and purpose, you will also be able to decide what information to include on your new online profile. I do encourage you to consider a similar look and feel for all of your profiles, unless you are specializing in more than one area (for instance, art and science). You may like to use the same high quality square photo, logo, description, website address, email address, mobile/cell phone number etc and remember once again to record your username and password in your usernames and passwords list.

Make sure you add relevant links as often as you can – sometimes these are 'follow' links and sometimes they are 'no follow' links. The best links for your search engine optimization strategy are 'follow links' – which essentially means that when internet search engines look at your profile, they record the links attached to your profile and index the relevant content.

Unfortunately I see many people who do not have consistent Platform Profiles – especially if they are a member of a Professional Association. This is such a waste! If your association membership entitles you to an online profile, this is FANTASTIC for attracting opportunities to you – so please take the time to fill in your profile and keep it up to date with all of the extra fields that can be completed.

You may also be required to add in the details of your professional development activities completed, events attended etc – again, find out what you need to update on a regular basis and make sure you do update your profile on a regular basis.

If you have a habit of checking all of your profiles at least once a year, you can also find out if there are more features that have been added to the platform. You can then take advantage of these opportunities. Many search results within a platform rely on recently updated information – so if you joined three years ago and haven't done anything since, you run the very real risk of not appearing in potential employer or client search results.

You may also like to have a Platform Profile on a globally recognized Avatar website like http://gravatar.com – this gives you an opportunity to update one profile that updates several other profiles. When you create your profiles, also add in all of your email addresses to each profile – that way you avoid the risk of duplicate profiles being established.

Once you have completed your profile, check and see what it looks like online – you may wish to adjust it in some way. If you haven't already, please consider creating a Google Profile at http://plus.google.com and adding in the Links section the links to all of your other Platform Profiles and websites. This is a way to talk directly to Google and help Google find you online (and likewise, the people considering you for a career or business opportunity).

Action 78: *Complete each chosen Platform Profile for your purpose but be consistent, be careful (so that you don't accidentally choose the wrong options) and add the full list of platforms to your Google+ Profile in the Links section*

12.2 Maximizing Each Platform

You will quickly discover that every platform operates slightly differently. You must start with a reasonably good quality profile (with as many sections completed as possible) – I call this your 'real estate' and you probably also need to review and select your security settings (although these can change without notice).

To really gain the most from a platform, you need to be active on the platform. Each platform will have a way for you to participate. You may be like the majority of users and just be a listener (or a lurker). You might choose to be an influencer and contribute new content. You might choose to be a participant and give feedback or make comments. You may like to be a little more public by regularly 'liking' content or a little more private by simply 'following' content.

Each platform has different algorithms that reward certain behaviors. Some of the behaviors score more 'brownie points' than others. For example, Likes are good, but Shares are usually excellent. One behavior could trigger an automatic beneficial consequence and share your details to others.

Understanding what works for each platform will give you a greater chance of maximizing the platform. However, what works today may not work tomorrow! Every platform is trying to provide the best features for users (and remain financially viable). New features are regularly added and some old features are removed. What may have been extremely effective in the past could be removed simply because spammers ruined the opportunity and annoyed too many users so the platform provider had to change the platform to stop the bad behavior.

Some users blame the platform provider for the changes. Sometimes this is justified and other times, it is just a consequence of an increase in the volume of users. For example, LinkedIn originally notified all of your Connections when you published a Post, but now that so many people write Posts, they only notify selected Connections.

New platforms also create new features and then existing platforms incorporate the new features into their platform. An obvious example of this is hashtags – these originally came from Twitter but you can now use hashtags in many other platforms.

Some platforms also offer a Premium Service and some users complain that they have to 'Pay to Play.' I always suggest that you make sure you have made maximum use of the Freemium Service before you pay for the Premium Service.

If the Premium Service does lead to the business or career opportunities you desire, what is wrong with paying for this feature? If it is not leading to those opportunities, there is often no point in continuing to pay for the feature, unless it is part of your overall brand strategy (for example, a part of your profession or industry membership where there is no Freemium Service).

Many people assume that they can 'fill in the boxes' and they don't need any professional assistance to maximize the platform. I disagree. I think most people can understand basic features and benefits and learn by experience and from other online content.

However, there are experts out there who can really show you the ins and outs of a particular platform and an hour or two of personalized coaching could see you increase your business and career attraction capacity significantly. They may even provide a simple review for a very small cost. Before hiring them, ask for details of their past successes and consider contacting one or two of their past clients to verify the potential results. Make sure you also have a good look at their profile and see if it matches their purpose!

Action 79: *Each platform has unique features and benefits that you can utilize for your purpose. Make sure your activity is aligned with the career or business opportunities you wish to attract and consider hiring a platform specialist to identify additional specific strategies that will maximize your attraction capacity*

12.3 Measuring Your Platform Performance

I usually suggest that it takes about six months before you can really see the benefit of your activity in an online platform. It takes about this long for other users to have a sense of what you offer and how you are going to contribute. It will also take some time for you to test and experiment with various options and measure the results.

What you must do from the beginning is start with some baseline statistics. Record the numbers associated with your profile (number of connections, views, followers, following). Make a note when something special happens (lots of likes, comments or shares). Seek feedback from other users of the platform. See how others have performed over time (peers, leaders or competitors). Set a regular schedule for monitoring your performance (at least once every six months).

You may also like to take some screen shots (I use a Google Chrome Extension called 'Full Page Screen Capture') and save these in a relevant folder on your computer or the Cloud. You may like to record your statistics in a Spreadsheet so that you can track them over time and gain additional insights into what really works well for you.

By working out ways to measure your platform performance, you can develop your own personalized strategies and limit the amount of time you could potentially waste using a particular platform.

For example, a businesswoman posted a recent personal photo on Facebook and all of her friends started commenting on how her appearance 'hadn't changed in years.' So then she started posting more personal photos. This activity wasn't aligned with her business strategy so she was encouraged to think about what sort of content would lead to new business. Her friends already knew that she worked in real estate.

Her business is naturally very visual (different properties across the city), so she created business profiles on Pinterest and Instagram. Interestingly, Pinterest proved to be a waste of time and did not lead to any meaningful results. Instagram took off and was very successful. If she had not tried both platforms and measured the results, she would not have attracted new business opportunities.

People seeking career opportunities need to find out which platforms attract there target audience decision makers. There are often portals related to an industry or profession as well as individual company websites (with a careers section), specialist recruiters, headhunters and even discussion forums around interest areas. Participating in these forums can lead to referrals from existing members or you may simply arouse the interest of lurkers who notice a quality comment and then track you down. Gone are the days when you had to wait for a job to be advertised in the newspaper – there are now thousands of ways to attract a career opportunity.

Action 80: *Measuring and monitoring your platform performance can help you work out what works and is worth pursuing and what doesn't work and needs to be reconsidered*

12.4 Platform Power Tools

Every platform has a unique way of encouraging users to engage with its resources. In this section, I would like to share a few tips and tricks you may like to experiment with:

- **Google Plus and Google My Business (formerly Google+ Local, Google Places and Google Maps)** – Google is trying to list Google content in search results before paid advertisements and organic search results – so making sure that you have all of your information on these profiles is essential. You can boost your performance even further if you regularly add photos, videos and additional content. This is particularly important if most of your target audience users their mobile/cell phone to find your details

- **LinkedIn** – on your personal profile, your headline (directly under your name) is your top search criteria location. Optimizing your entire profile with your keywords is essential and if you are connected to more people in your area of expertise, this also helps you appear in those expertise search results. LinkedIn also likes you to be relatively active – allow at least five minutes per week to complete a relevant activity. Your company profile should also share an update at least once a month and your employees and key stakeholders should be encouraged to like and share your updates

- **Facebook** – is tracking everything that you do, look at etc so if you are missing out on seeing the content you want, make sure you go to that Facebook Page and 'turn on' Notifications so that you do see the Updates even if you don't click on them every time. Messages sent via your personal profile have a much wider reach than those sent via a Facebook Page or Group

- **Twitter** – I find that one of the best uses of Twitter is collecting information from thought leaders in the areas I am most interested in. They now share video content and this is also quite effective at generating engagement. Senior executives who share interesting content can actually affect the share price of the enterprise – so setting a good example from the top can be very helpful to an enterprise

- **Instagram** – as this is owned by Facebook, there are many integrations with Facebook that are helping Instagram expand at a rapid rate. With only one link on each account, it is a little more difficult to generate traffic to a website but it can connect like information via hashtags. I personally find that it attracts a lot of fake likes. Probably more suited to anyone with a very visual career or business focus

- **Pinterest** – with a high proportion of female users, Pinterest initially helped generate a trend towards more visual online content. If you have a passion in a particular area, it is possible to find like-minded people and share your images and ideas internationally. In my view, it hasn't developed sufficiently to maintain ongoing interest and the audience numbers do not appear to be growing exponentially

- **Forums**- various online forums have been around for a very long time, even before social media took off. They are more likely to be used by people interested in technology or specific audiences (like international expatriates or community support forums). Some large organizations have internal forums (Yammer looks very similar to Facebook but it is only available for an enterprise). Forums usually need to have good moderators to maintain interest and keep noisy or nuisance contributors under control. To get the most out of forums, you need to access them reasonably frequently. I find that some people can become quite addicted to forums or alternatively, sign up and never do anything else so they miss the opportunity to gain any real value. A lot of professional bodies have closed their individual forums and created mainstream groups on more popular forums (like LinkedIn or Facebook)

- **Messaging Systems** – email marketing has traditionally been very effective, but more and more young people are not looking at their emails at all. SMS messages appear to receive a greater response rate but having a conversation with multiple people via text message can be complex. A number of large companies are using Facebook to help manage staff shift swaps and availability notifications because they are aware that most young people have a Facebook account and this is a platform that they already know how to use. Understanding which method is more likely to generate a response is important when thinking about how you can attract interest in what you are offering

- **Apps** – for years there have been jokes about there being 'an app for that.' I have found that one of the biggest challenges with apps is the ability to provide the full experience that the customer requires. The best apps appear to be constantly improved and enhanced. If the first experience of an app is poor, it can be very difficult to re-generate interest in the app in the future (particularly relevant for apps that require content to be added after the app is developed and especially when there is very little data in the app on launch date). When you realize that a lot of content in the future will be sourced by a voice command to a mobile device, unless the app can be utilized with this type of search, there is a chance that many apps could be bypassed forever unless they are integrated with wearable technology

Ultimately, if you find a useful platform or you are encouraged to utilize a particular tool, you will need to investigate the pros and cons thoroughly. Ideally, try and sit down with an experienced user and have the best features for your purpose demonstrated to you. Be constantly willing to explore the latest features and improvements but again, don't get side-tracked by the latest 'shiny object' – stick to your purpose and choose the options that will help you attract the right career or business.

Action 81: *Every platform or tool will have a range of features that will either help you attract the right career or business or keep you distracted from attracting the right career or business. Be discerning and see if you can find an experienced user to show you the best features for your purpose*

12.5 Game Changers

As time goes by, the rules of the game change and the actual game itself changes. Here are some trends that are altering the status quo in significant ways.

- **Ad Blocking Software** – as users become more and more frustrated by the amount of ads appearing on their screens, ad blocking software is designed to try and counter the effect. This is a serious concern for businesses that rely on advertisements to attract their target audience

- **Aggregator Services** – when most enterprises in a sector are aggregated on a larger portal, it leaves the enterprises who are not included in the portal at a severe disadvantage. The portal also has the potential to drive the profit margin even lower as they are skimming a fee for simply aggregating the information electronically but not providing actual products or services and incurring the costs of running a business

- **Everything for free** – more and more people are expecting to access information for free and pay the lowest price possible for any personal service. There has been a trend away from paying for professional association membership, paying local country taxes and levies and maintaining living wages and employment benefits. On the other hand, people are often willing to pay an exorbitant amount for something that has a perceived value (thanks to clever marketing and publicity). Whilst more people are able to access basic goods and services, there is a small group of people across the world that hold a majority of the financial wealth and this creates disharmony, particularly in countries where there is a large population of extremely poor people

- **Personalization** – more and more content and services are being designed for individuals rather than communities. Whereas past generations would develop a general understanding across a range of topics and skills, individuals are now able to personally select what content they receive within a very narrow niche (either by choice or predictive artificial intelligence). In my view, this process has the ability to isolate people and reduce their ability to participate in collective activities or help them understand others

- **Mass Manipulation** – now that data has been collected for some years and data scientists have learnt how to interpret that data, we are in a position where artificial intelligence and predictive analysis could easily be used for the wrong reasons. There needs to be a system in place that provides an ethical barrier to any form of mass manipulation. In the past, selected individuals held power over countries and media publications. Nowadays, there are many channels to share a message and enable people to work for the greater good. That said, we still need to be aware that these same systems that allow the sharing of good works also have the potential to share bad works

Understanding that these game changers can have a significant influence on our future means that we can think about the attraction techniques we could use and how their performance may be affected. Again, if you focus on attraction techniques that have a lifetime and a dynamic value, you should be able to remain relevant and findable for your target audience. By being aware and alert to sudden changes, you can adjust your attraction strategy.

The one strategy that I believe will always remain relevant is the networking strategy. As you probably already know, the quality of your network can often be equated to your personal net worth. If you have a number of resources in different areas and you keep them connected to you, if one 'link' is broken, you can still rely on the rest of the network to support you. If you live in a linear fashion and the road changes direction, you may not be able to change your path quickly enough. A wider network also reduces your risk, particularly if there are several resource hubs (alternative sources of income or support).

Action 82: *Be aware that at any point in the future, there could be a significant change in the way that careers develop or businesses operate. By developing a networking strategy and multiple resource hubs, you have a greater ability to attract the right career or business and adjust to any changes in the marketplace*

13. Process Attraction Techniques

Once you have established good quality real estate in a variety of online and offline platforms, you can now move forward with a range of specific strategies to attract the right career or business opportunity. Identifying, selecting and completing these processes will lead to new opportunities.

Action 83: *Process attraction techniques will help you continually find, select and complete activities that lead to new opportunities*

13.1 Finding Advertised Opportunities

There are many places to apply for advertised opportunities. There are:

- job aggregator websites that combine listings for individual job / career websites
- individual job / career websites
- organization websites (for profit and not-for-profit) and viewable by the public
- organization intranets and not viewable by the public
- industry associations
- professional associations
- freelancer, outsourcer, contracting portals
- tender portals
- niche information portals
- online forums
- community noticeboards – libraries, universities, shops etc
- newspapers, magazines, journals
- recruitment firms
- social media
- business brokers and seller listings
- auction, trading, events and classified advertisement listings

Although many jobs are never officially advertised, you can see from this list that there are multiple places where you can find an opportunity or share your story to attract the right career or business.

Let me share some examples.

A local real estate firm never advertises an official position as vacant, they simply announce on their Facebook page that they would like to have a new person on their sales team.

A small business that likes to set up stands at local markets and fetes approaches groups who advertise their upcoming events to see if they can apply for a stand.

An English language tutor puts up a small notice at the local library where a large percentage of international students study every day.

A single mother in the Philippines quits her day job to look after her young son and puts her profile on various freelancer websites so that she can attract and apply for roles from a different time zone so that she can work when her son is at school or sleeping.

If you ask 10 people how they found their last three jobs, I am sure you will soon have even more suggestions about how to find an advertised (or non-advertised) opportunity.

Action 84: *Look beyond traditional career or business advertisement listings and find new locations for the potential career or business opportunity you are seeking*

13.2 Applying For Advertised Opportunities

Unfortunately I have heard countless stories from people who have applied for hundreds of jobs or business opportunities and they have told me that they have been unsuccessful and therefore:

- they must be too old, too young, too good, too bad etc
- they must be too educated or not educated enough
- there must be too many people applying
- the system must be rigged
- it is because they don't have any local experience

- their business is too small or too big
- they charge too much or not enough
- the decision maker didn't like their name or photo or some other personal characteristic
- or some other excuse (one person suggested to me it was because they came from Tibet!)

I may sound a little flippant here but I am trying to make a very serious point. If you are not getting to the first stage of a career or business opportunity (an interview or a meeting), then the information you have supplied does not answer the decision maker's questions adequately.

I have found that in most cases, it is because the person applying for the advertised opportunity tries to use exactly the same information for every single opportunity. This means that the decision maker has to interpret your information and make sense of how it applies to the opportunity and this takes effort. If someone else has tailored their information, they are much more likely to be considered and added to the short list.

So you need to put yourself in the shoes of the decision maker. If you were in their position, what information would you want to see? How would you like to receive that information? If there was any additional information included, would that add or detract from your application?

The skills to find and secure a career or business opportunity are DIFFERENT to the skills to carry out the tasks within that career or business opportunity.

Essentially what I am sharing with you here are search and application techniques.

Here are some general tips:

- make sure you include everything that they asked for
- leave out anything that is not relevant or could detract from your application

- make sure you only use plain text and bold formatting as Applicant Tracking Systems (ATS) do not like fancy formatting in resumes or CV's

- be consistent in your layout and have correct spelling and grammar

- be prompt and follow up as required

- do not lie and make sure that you appropriately explain any date gaps (in your career history – you can massage the message here to sound more positive than negative)

- consider finding out more specific inside information before applying so that you can include information that may support your application in a unique and positive way

- keep an accurate record and filing system so that when you are contacted, you can quickly and easily find a copy of what you have sent

- always say thank you, even if you miss out and invite the person to contact you again if another career or business opportunity becomes available

- diary for follow up about one month after the final process has been completed to see if any other opportunities are available. Consider doing this again three and six months later, particularly if there is the potential for a future career or business opportunity aligned with your values and purpose

What will always work is consistency and persistence. If one process doesn't work, try another or improve the process. Start with a smaller step before moving to a bigger step. If an opportunity doesn't exist, find a way to create one. Start with something voluntary and see where it leads. Meet people and network so that they can meet you and make a personal evaluation rather than try and interpret words on a screen or piece of paper. Ask for a referral.

If you have tried absolutely everything many times, in the absolute worst case scenario, consider moving to a location where you know that there are opportunities (this is always a last resort as I truly believe that with the right search skills, you can find an opportunity locally – you just need to be consistent, persistent and a bit flexible and patient).

I also believe that if two people with exactly the same skills and experience arrive in a new location on the same day, one person will always find a career or business opportunity before the other person – because they have better search and application skills, they are more consistent and persistent and they are flexible enough to do whatever it takes without making excuses.

Action 85: *When applying for a career or business opportunity, make sure that you include all of the information that has been requested in a format that is matched to the decision maker's needs. Be consistent and persistent in your approach and don't make excuses if something you have tried does not work.*

13.3 Passing the Application Process

If you have passed the first stage of the search and application process, the next stage is getting through the interview and assessment process. Some organizations will ask you to complete an assessment first, others may interview you over the telephone or in person first. Either way, it is all part of the process of getting to 'yes.'

As I have said before, if you are not getting to the interview stage, your application has not convinced the decision maker of the value you can provide. If you are receiving interviews and still not receiving a 'yes,' the most likely reason is that the decision maker did not see a 'cultural fit' between you and the career or business opportunity.

There are also other reasons as to why you may have missed out:

- you may have arrived late
- you may have dressed inappropriately for their preference
- you may have a different body language style that was misinterpreted or not in alignment with their personal preferences – not enough smiling, too much smiling, not enough eye contact, too much eye contact etc
- you did not answer the questions adequately
- you did not demonstrate enough knowledge about the career or business opportunity
- you gave too little or too much information
- you appeared desperate for the opportunity (you need to be relaxed and willing to walk out without the opportunity regardless of your personal circumstances)

- you didn't connect with the decision maker (for a completely obvious or completely unknown reason)
- you provided information that was in conflict with their values and beliefs
- there was another candidate who matched their requirements more closely
- they were only interviewing you because they 'had to' and they had already chosen someone else
- because they were hungry, it was Friday or some other equally ridiculous reason

Regardless of the reason why you missed out, or the reason they told you why you missed out (sometimes they will give you a 'safe' answer so that you will not pursue legal action when that may not be the real reason at all), you need to be willing to move on and not take it personally (unless there really is something you need to work on – for example, arriving on time). In most cases, you will never know the real reason so it is pointless trying to find out or give it a label.

There are various ways to build your resilience throughout this phase:

- celebrate reaching this stage each time it occurs
- recognize what you did well and what you learnt
- realize that for each second stage you get to, you are closer to the third successful stage
- if not this opportunity, then something better in the future
- if they didn't like you from the beginning, then it may not have worked out in the end
- there are other people who value you just as you are
- you can still follow up and be considered for a future opportunity
- you are still working on several other opportunities and this was good practice

You probably know what else you need to do to keep yourself motivated and positive through this stage based on your own personality preferences (chocolate comes to my mind!). Remember to spend most of your time with people who will encourage you, not people who will just whine with you. Take immediate positive action, even if you don't feel like it – a step forward is always better than a step back. You never know what is just around the corner and this experience could be the catalyst for a career or business opportunity that is more closely aligned to your values and purpose.

Action 86: *Always do your best in interviews and meetings, but do not stress about the reasons why you may have missed out on the career or business opportunity. Simply relax and keep moving forward and do what you need to do to maintain your resilience, consistence and persistence*

13.4 Starting A Career Or Business Opportunity

On the first day of a new career or business opportunity, it is fairly normal to feel a certain level of pressure. This stress can make you more alert and receptive to the new information or it can make you feel a little overwhelmed. If you are starting a new career, the onboarding or induction process may be very comprehensive or completely non-existent. If you are starting out in business, you may have already completed an enormous amount of work and this first day is simply the culmination of many other days prior to today.

Before you began the journey to this new opportunity, you were unconsciously incompetent in relation to every aspect of the role. As you started to move towards the role, you realized that you were consciously incompetent, at least in some aspects of the role. This is also what happens on day one and I believe it usually takes at least six months before you become fully consciously competent and it can take even longer to become unconsciously competent – where what you do each day feels like second nature or automatic pilot – you don't have to think about what you are doing.

So when you are starting from a position of 'consciously incompetent,' it is very easy to make mistakes and these first impressions can have a short term or a long term effect. I therefore suggest that you find ways to manage your learning and risks during this period of high intensity. You must, in every situation, keep yourself safe and not be afraid to ask questions to maintain your personal safety (particularly if you are working with machinery or in a potentially dangerous situation).

If things do go wrong, be willing to apologize and make amends. Make every effort to learn and improve, even if this requires extra effort in your own time. Most employers and customers will accept your mistakes if you show them that you are willing to fix them. I personally prefer to start with an attitude of learning and understanding the status quo rather than arriving and changing everything from the beginning (even if I was asked to do so). As soon as I do understand the environment, I then look at ways to improve my own performance and assist others if I can – however, I can assure you that this is not always welcome – some people like things to stay exactly the same!

Workplaces and marketplaces have their own nuances and understanding these can help you in your career in business. Constantly look for clues and information to help you understand what works. If you have any involvement with people, I encourage you to consider the 'fun, food and free' methodology.

Most people like things that are fun, include food and are free of charge. I regularly encourage new employees to bring food to work to share (but not too regularly otherwise people expect it!). I also encourage new employees to participate in work social functions and also invite people to join you for a free drink (non-alcoholic) or activity close to work. You still need to maintain your own private social life, but the occasional friendly activity with your work colleagues can help you in your career.

The same applies in business. If your clients or customers have fun, receive food and the extra benefits are free of charge, they too are likely to enjoy the opportunity. The only proviso here is that you are not seen to be bribing anyone (very important in relation to working with government and corporate organizations and meeting governance requirements).

It is also important to start collecting records of your achievements. Regardless of how long you are in the career or business, you will need to document these in your online profile or resume as it is very easy to forget if you do not keep a record as you go.

Action 87: *Start every career or business opportunity with an attitude of learning and understanding and start keeping records so that you can use this information in the future for your next steps*

13.5 Daily Career And Business Strategies

When you are in the right career or business, every day feels like a blessing. You wake up and you know that you are living your values and your purpose. You still accept that there will be challenges, life has its usual ups and downs, but overall, you know that life is great and that your gifts are being shared effectively.

If you are still working towards the right career or business, there are daily strategies that you can implement to help attract more aligned opportunities in the future. You can:

- acknowledge and celebrate what is aligned right now
- identify what needs to be improved and do something about it (even if it is just a few small items before you tackle the big items)
- complete some steps towards your future goals and aspirations on a part time and low cost basis
- manage the challenges of your current situation and change your view of the circumstances (perhaps some aspects are only a perception and a new view will change your attitude)
- seek some extra support or help to deal with your current situation or move you towards a future destination
- be grateful for every single blessing you have at this moment
- accept that some aspects may not be possible to change for now and you will just have to work around them in the immediate short term

If you want to attract the right career or business opportunity, you need to lay the foundation. It doesn't have to be a fully excavated and channeled site, but there needs to be a space where it can be created. You need to focus on what you want and not on what you don't want. A clear vision will help you move towards what you want and ignore what is not aligned (for example, if you want red bricks, you wouldn't even look at brown bricks would you?).

If you write down what you want to achieve, it becomes more defined and tangible and you can review it on a more regular basis (and tick off what you have achieved). You can do some additional research and find out whether or not your aspirations are realistic –

or even unrealistic but still possible. Be willing to be bold and step outside of your comfort zone. Be willing to give before receiving. Expand your vision and always be willing to learn more. People who are happy with their career or business are much more likely to be happy in life.

Also be aware of the 'happiness trap.' The all-pervading will to be 'happy' that means you end up feeling unhappy if you are not happy all the time. For years, people have cried for 'world peace.' My cry is for 'world contentment.' It is similar to happiness, but it includes an element of satisfaction – of allowing the mind to be quiet and accepting of the current state of being. If we are constantly striving or fighting, how can we possibly feel peace or contentment? For me, world peace requires other people to make a commitment to peace. World contentment allows every one of us as an individual to find our own level and share our unique gifts.

Some people actually enjoy striving all the time and this helps our society grow and develop. Others are prepared to defend and protect us and this keeps us safe. In my view, a harmonious society is based on diversity and ethical flexibility, not conformity and dictatorial rigidity.

Action 88: *Find ways every day to live according to your values and purpose, even if your current situation is not completely aligned. Take action steps to develop the foundation for your future and be content with what you have achieved right now*

13.6 Education And Learning Based Strategies

To survive in the modern world, we need to be lifelong learners. It is no longer possible for us to complete some form of schooling and then an apprenticeship or trade and trust that it will last for the next 50 years. Every single career and business is growing and changing over time.

There are many ways to learn new information. Some people find that the only way they can learn is if someone shows them how to do something live and in person and then they practice it immediately and perfect it over time.

There is a huge amount of information available online and I have heard of all sorts of handymen looking up YouTube videos to find out how to do something by watching someone else doing it on the screen. Other people prefer detailed written instructions. Others prefer just a few short clues and to work it out themselves.

One thing I do want to encourage you to consider is informal education. Some of us have been programmed to believe that unless we receive our education from a formal institution, it is not valid. Other people believe that the only education worth receiving is real life experience. What I believe is that we simply need to find ways to be constantly learning and not cutting off any of these opportunities. Let's consider a few different sources of learning:

- formal qualifications through a school, college or university
- apprenticeships and vocational courses
- qualification and certification programs
- specific programs for people with some form of disadvantage (age, disability, long term unemployment etc)
- faith, community and local learning centers
- business enterprises offering free or low cost introduction sessions
- social justice groups offering tailored programs
- training organizations offering short courses (live or online)
- professional associations offering events, masterclasses, professional development workshops and conferences
- mentoring programs
- self-directed learning – audio, video, online, books etc (you could even borrow these from a local library)
- individual groups that meet regularly and have guest speakers or short courses
- volunteers (including family and friends) who are simply willing to help
- the internet and apps – websites, social media, portals, forums, gamification learning etc

If you start to think of learning in this much broader sense, you will soon see that there are so many different ways that you can learn and attract the right career or business into your life. You do not necessarily have to attend an Ivy League university and obtain an MBA or PhD to achieve your goals. Your situation is not hopeless even if you didn't finish school or you haven't completed any formal study for several years. It is never too late to start learning and it doesn't have to cost a fortune. Even old dogs can learn new tricks, they just have to learn one trick at a time. Don't let a qualification stop you from moving towards your goals.

Action 89: *To attract the right career or business opportunity, you need to be a lifelong learner. There are many free and low cost ways to learn new information and skills and it is never too late to start learning*

13.7 Proactive Action Strategies

Whilst I was still at secondary school, I secured two job interviews and both companies offered me a job. In my first job, I was interviewed for a role as a Training Officer and I was offered the job (three out of three isn't bad!). When I was successful the third time, I asked the interviewer why I got the job and he said, it was because I was 'proactive.' That word has stuck in my head ever since.

Your family background and culture is likely to affect how comfortable you are about putting yourself forward for opportunities. If you don't like 'putting yourself out there,' you may have found the title of this book appealing because in theory, the opportunity would be attracted to you.

However, it doesn't just happen. You need to give your target audience clues that you are interested. They need to be able to find your information and contact you. They need to see you often enough to be comfortable making a career or business decision.

If you are using a content based strategy, your articles or online profiles are the seeds that you have planted. When this information is promoted (either automatically or with some assistance), the roots are spread. When someone finds this information, they see the plant that has grown. If they make a career or business decision, they are collecting the fruit.

As I have stated several times, you need to have a multi-channel and multi-media approach using multiple concurrent strategies to spread your risk and avoid the challenges of algorithm changes. You need to generate signals that can be picked up that lead to some level of engagement. You want to have digital and non-digital assets that generate results for a lifetime and remain current and relevant as a result of your dynamic activity. You want to avoid paying for every opportunity and you want to generate the best return for essentially, the least effort.

So you need to be proactive and you need to choose the best strategies for your purpose. What will work for you could be completely different to what will work for someone else. You may want to assume because one technique worked, it will always work. You may also assume that a technique won't work and therefore, not give it any consideration.

As a general rule, I like to use techniques that provide maximum effect. I simply do not have the time to try everything and I certainly do not have time to waste. I prefer to work with lifetime value options and maintain just enough dynamic value options to remain relevant and current and not create the wrong impression or perception.

I don't always get it right and yes, I have made a few small mistakes. On balance though, by being proactive, I have sourced some wonderful opportunities.

I have also had to keep sourcing new opportunities even when I am working on existing opportunities. This is a common trap in business. The business owner goes all out promoting their goods and services and then ends up so busy that they don't have any time for marketing – and then they run out of work because they weren't doing any marketing! You need to keep a fairly consistent balance between working on the business (or career) and in the business (or career).

On some occasions, I have probably ended up with a little too much to do all at once. I have had to again be proactive and either pass on the work to other people or find someone to help me do the work myself. As I am a bit of a 'lone ranger' in business and I like to do most of the work myself, I have chosen to pass the work on to others (without requesting a referral fee). I see this as a way of giving back to the market for the referrals that I have received (also without paying a referral fee).

Let's look at some specific actions you can take to help attract the right career or business opportunity. You can:

- participate in discussions by liking, commenting and sharing content that is related to your ideal career or business

- maintain an interesting social media presence so that people can discover and learn more about your target career or business (but limit the number of sales messages to almost zero)

- send out broadcast messages on special occasions or produce quirky viral messages that people want to share

- do something completely unique – checkout http://www.rleonardi.com/interactive-resume/ or http://nina4airbnb.com to see how these people have used their existing skills to demonstrate to future employers what they have to offer (if the links no longer work, visit http://archive.org and look at a former version from May 2016)

- start Following thought leaders and responding to their latest broadcasts with Likes, Comments and Shares. Comment on other people's comments

- re-post good quality links and content through your platform profiles and include relevant tags so that you can attract like-minded people

- keep up to date with trends and maintain a consistent technology updating schedule. I tend to wait until the bugs are ironed out of new equipment or software before I upgrade – by adopting a little later, I also save some costs because the price usually drops a little as competition increases. A good example of this is cars – the first release of a new model is usually quite exciting, but the second release has been adjusted based on customer feedback and is usually even better than the first edition

- consider paying for a professional membership, selected advertising or business systems, particularly if they generate brand awareness or direct sales even though there is an initial expense. A good example of this is my online newsletter service. In the past, I would spend up to three hours a month removing unsubscribes and adding new subscriptions. It is not cheap to have this done automatically, but I can assure you, it saves me time and headaches!

- participate in a job search program so that you can acquire more job search skills and network with the other participants

- secure a work experience placement in an aligned organization, industry or profession so that people can see you in action and provide you with referrals

- get involved with a club or group related to your career or business (or with the target audience you want to attract)

- connect with a faith or religious group (if that is your interest) and become involved in their outreach programs, advisory boards or leadership roles

- attend community events in your local area and start talking to people. Door knock local businesses and offer your services on a short term voluntary basis or deliver an introduction letter explaining what you have to offer and how they can contact you (including a special limited time offer – like the first three hours free)

- set up an account management matrix so that you approach finding a job as thoroughly as managing a significant project

- utilize various online job search or business startup guides (these can save you hours of time and stop you reinventing the wheel!)

- hire a career development professional or suitably qualified business advisor to help you make wise choices, select suitable actions and complete agreed tasks

- find a way to create a job – by starting on a voluntary, temporary or part time basis and then help the decision maker come to a conclusion that you would be a valuable asset to the business and accept more duties as time goes on

- start applying for promotions and letting your supervisor know that you are interested in more challenging work or new duties

Once again, if you asked 10 people for their top three proactive action strategies that helped them find a great career or business opportunity, I am sure that you will find that there are many unique and interesting ways to attract opportunities.

Action 90: *There are many ways that you can be proactive both online and offline to generate signals to your target audience that you are interested in a career or business opportunity. You need to adopt a multi-channel, multi-media approach using multiple concurrent strategies and select the best options for your purpose*

13.8 System Based Strategies

If you want to continually attract repeated opportunities, at some point you won't want to do it all manually any more, you will want to be able to automate and replicate the process, possibly without any level of interaction.

You will essentially be creating a very specific product for a very specific target audience and you will be relying on a system or process to attract the one off or repeated opportunity.

Some people will tell you that they never had to apply for a job because the job always found them – this means that they have a system in place (either intentional or unintentional) that is generating the opportunities for them. They have planted enough seeds, nurtured enough plants and collected the ripe fruits.

Businesses can offer either time based services, value based services or value based products.

Small businesses offering time based services can find it very difficult to increase their revenue because there are only 24 hours in a day and as a small business, they do not have very many staff to make their operation scalable. In many cases, they are essentially self-employed – because a business is only a business if it is scalable. If a business is scalable, it has the potential to last longer because it is not relying on just a few key people working manually to survive.

Good systems and processes have the ability to help individuals create a scalable business. By charging for value instead of time, a business can increase their scalability. By increasing their product sales (provided they keep their production and distribution costs under control), they can also increase their scalability.

To attract more business, the business owners need to have the right 'wheel hub' with spokes to help the wheel continue turning. That means multiple methods for generating business. Some businesses try and combine both products and services so that they can have a larger hub and multiple income streams. Savvy business owners select reliable spokes that direct the right target audience directly to the business. They may also develop new categories to stay one step ahead of the competition and they know how to reach the hot button of buyers by satisfying their biggest fears or desires.

As mentioned previously, higher end products can sell better and may have a slightly longer life-span – but this is still not a guarantee for success – especially when some very lucrative businesses survive on a profit margin of just 5%. Ultimately, I would suggest that business owners will want to be able to develop a reliable asset that generates a sustainable income and has a reasonable market value within three to five years of starting out. During that time, the business will try and product-ization and customer-ization the enterprise – by developing congruent replicable systems.

Let's have a look at some of the marketing channels (or wheel spokes) that can systematically drive the right target audience to a career or business opportunity:

- events, conferences, expos and exhibitions – these are a great way to introduce you or your business to a target audience
- awards – the process of entering awards, becoming a finalist, winning an award and promoting the award win
- competitions – encourage people to take a small risk and be open to a new opportunity and can feed into internal marketing systems
- memberships – which create an ongoing relationship and recurring revenue opportunities
- sponsorships and alliances – in cash or in kind – these are great tools for providing reciprocal value with like-minded individuals or enterprises
- assessments – certifications, authorizations, regulations can all add credibility but also improve operating procedures
- networks – either individual, industry or profession based can increase branding and awareness and lead to excellent cross fertilization of ideas and opportunities
- webinars – allowing people to access information from the comfort of their home or workplace
- video – allowing anytime access to pre-recorded details
- auto-responder and landing page systems – using if this, then that sequences from initial contact through to final sale, in conjunction with customer relationship management (CRM) systems, databases, social media etc

- apps – that engage and inform and prompt predictive options based on past behavior

I would like to reiterate, all of these options can be considered for individuals seeking career opportunities as well as businesses wanting to attract more sales. Individuals can simply consume these items or actively seek them – for example, obtaining a professional Certification can give you extra credibility and help attract better employment offers as well as make you stand out above other candidates.

What I like about system based strategies is that once they are set up and have been completed the first time, they are usually relatively easy to maintain. The reason many people do not attract opportunities is because they are not prepared to make an investment up front.

Yes, it takes time and energy to implement a new accounting system or produce a good quality video (especially if you hate being in front of the camera). But once these resources are established, they can be used over and over again, to your advantage and once you have gone through the process once, the second time around it will be a lot easier.

Action 91: *Although establishing a system based strategy for attracting career or business opportunities may take some initial time to set up, the potential rewards can be greater. Select the systems that will add the most value to your career or business goals*

14. Possibility Attraction Techniques

There are some people who believe that anything is possible and other people who think that nothing is possible. If you would like to open yourself up to the world of possibility, you need to be willing to look beyond your nose. To see the potential in an opportunity, not just the pitfalls.

You also need to think about probability. If the probability is extremely low, do you want to take the risk? If the probability is high, would you still push on if you were busy right now? Or would you wait until a better time?

Some of us feel comfortable doing things immediately, some of us need to warm up first. Some people like to assess risk and have all of the facts and figures first, others will push on with just a sniff of a chance.

Do you generally act or react when a possibility is presented to you? Do you respond immediately or do you ignore it instantly? How much detail do you actually hear when the possibility is first presented to you and do you ask further questions for clarification?

If you want to attract possibilities, you need to be flexible and willing to take action – either immediately or at a defined point in the future. Part of your response can involve conducting further research – it doesn't mean that you automatically accept every possibility.

People who can make a decision after they have assessed the risk and then carry out the necessary actions have the greatest chance of securing good possibilities. Don't assume that you have not had any possibilities in the past, you may have simply missed them because they were not obvious to you at the time.

Action 92: *When you are presented with a possibility, take a moment to investigate your options and consider the opportunity. Be willing to take action based on research, probability and an appropriate risk assessment*

14.1 Traditional Possibility Sources

Over time, we have become accustomed to hearing about possibilities from certain people or initiatives. These can include:

- the grapevine – at work or university
- government initiatives – for example missions to develop international trade or regional development projects
- industry initiatives – often prompted by changing market conditions or influence from the main players in a specific industry
- long standing relationships – with school friends, university or employer alumni, colleagues
- serendipity – simply being in the right place at the right time
- personal development – as you grow, so does the flow
- completely out of the blue from nowhere – no-one can explain it but all of a sudden, something just happens
- a deep conversation – that goes beyond normal chit chat and leads to a direct referral

I believe that possibilities are created when we increase our awareness. When we look beyond what we already know and we adopt an inquisitive approach to life and living. When we have a willingness to explore and seek out new adventures and better ways of doing what we already do.

Action 93: *To attract more possibilities in your career or business, increase your personal awareness of what is going on around you, be inquisitive and willing to explore new horizons*

14.2 Contemporary Possibility Sources

In some respects, possibilities are infinite. As every new system or process is designed, millions of variables become available. What initially started in one form quickly morphs into multiple opportunities with multiple possible consequences (good and bad).

Some contemporary possibilities are simply traditional possibilities that have been enhanced. Let's look at writing a book. Traditionally, it was a privilege only granted to the elite because they were the only ones who were taught to read. Now, you can self-publish a paperback or an e-book and use it like a business card to attract expensive consulting or speaking assignments.

A significant game changer has been the rise of databases – locations where multiple records are kept in one place and can easily be searched based on keywords and algorithms (including dates, keyword frequency, complex search strings and more). These can be internal databases in an enterprise or public databases like websites, resume listing services, social media profiles, professional or trade directories.

The nature of work has also changed in the last 100 years thanks to multiple factors, but in particular, the globalization of the workforce. The traditional employer and employee relationship is rapidly disappearing and market forces appear to be driving down labor costs in many countries, particularly where there is very little government regulation on pay and penalty rates. For work-life balance reasons, some people are choosing to work casually, part time or on a freelance basis and others are either choosing or being forced into contract, consulting or self-employment opportunities.

If you would like to find opportunities in this new environment, you need to find new methods. Here are a few suggestions:

- follow up on old advertisements that are still visible online – sometimes the first round of interest did not attract a decision maker, so you can get in before the advertisement is re-launched
- do your research and find out what is going on in an enterprise, an industry or a profession and make sure that you have the skills or talents that are in demand and then shop yourself around to the best enterprises
- start with a freelance assignment or a short term voluntary project so that you really make sure that the area you would like to explore is right for you
- understand the sharing economy and find out how to get involved at a basic level before making a full commitment (various platforms provide a way for you to attract your target audience for a small percentage transaction fee)
- collaborate with an existing brand or enterprise rather than start from scratch – if your dream is to have your own coffee shop, why not work for one first and find out what it is really like?

- join a collective so you all share the risk but you are still independent of each other – then you don't have complicated partnerships or legal entities to establish

- combine your marketing forces – perhaps you have a group of three friends and you all share a passion for working in the legal industry – perhaps you can take it in turns as to who goes to what events and then you report back to the group at regular intervals

- do something completely different part time for a while – disrupt your normal neural pathways and add a bit of variety and spice to your life

- review your current situation more objectively – perhaps the real reason you are trying to attract a new opportunity is because you want to avoid a person rather than find a new career or business (many people quit their job or their business because of one person that caused them challenges)

Action 94: *Explore how new systems and processes are creating possibilities to be found or work collaboratively, particularly if they involve you trialing and testing a new career or business opportunity before full implementation*

14.3 Speculative Possibility Sources

You may have heard the expression, "You have got to be in it to win it." There are a lot of people who miss possibilities because they only accept an opportunity if there is a high likelihood that it will lead to a successful outcome.

That is why some people cannot think beyond having a job – where they are paid every week or month for completing a task. A business owner may incur an expense and not receive a return for more than a year.

The same applies to possibilities. Some opportunities only appear when you put yourself out there and you do something for free first. It might be something you do on a voluntary basis as part of a community initiative or group or it could be something that you do in business hoping that it leads to something better. It could be a phone call, a meeting or a whole day or week preparing a significant tender document.

Here are some other ideas:

- start tutoring or teaching at a university or training organization (your students may need your professional paid assistance on top of the paid time you spend in class)

- be a guest speaker at events (that way your details are shared around the databases associated with the event)

- start up a group or network and host regular events (you will be the go-to person for further information)

- write an e-Book or White Paper that you offer to send to people you have met whilst networking

- re-connect with people from your past and keep them up to date on what you would like to do in the future

- speak to event organizers and centers of influence and ask for information on where you can go for further information and ideas

- talk to your neighbors – this is good for your mental health as well as your financial health

- provide consulting services part-time. I met a guy who was an expert in IT and he was working in a call center. Everyone knew he was an expert so they gave him a range of small jobs until he had enough jobs to leave the call center and start his own enterprise

- go where the movers and shakers are – another person I met got a job in a hotel and he would talk to the senior executives who stayed there to find out about opportunities and to source referrals

- attend selected events and ask if you can be a speaker next time – it is a lot easier to address everyone at once than it is to meet everyone individually (and your details will also be sent to the people who do not attend but still receive the invitation)

Action 95: *Be prepared to put yourself out there for a zero initial return, particularly if it puts your details in front of your key target audience*

14.4 Ongoing Possibility Sources

After so many years of attracting the right career and business opportunities, I have been able to distill the various techniques I have used and I have chosen the best techniques aligned with my values and purpose. I also keep my eyes open for any new techniques I would like to try and I also stop doing some activities that no longer deliver results.

Likewise, over time, you will find the best possibility sources for your values and purpose. There are a few criteria I use to assess which possibility sources I will continue to use:

- they may take some time to set up but the ongoing maintenance is relatively low
- they maintain my profile with my target audience
- they continue to generate my ideal career and business opportunities
- for the most part, I enjoy completing the associated tasks
- they are credible and reliable – enhancing my personal or business brand
- they combine traditional and contemporary methodologies
- they are authentic and ethical
- they pass yearly review and feedback processes
- they are not too time consuming or labor intensive
- they give a reasonable return on investment
- I like doing it and will continue anyway

The last point is an interesting one. Not everything provides a direct career or business benefit. However, due to the large number of hours I spend doing the work I love, there are some activities that I simply enjoy and I am happy to continue doing them because it is fun and it meets my social and personal needs. I don't mind spending a few extra minutes with a nice client here and there – or hosting a regular event that doesn't lead to any direct work because it is close to home and I see people I like and I always learn something new. However, as a percentage of my overall possibility attraction strategies, they are a small component.

Action 96: *Assess which possibility sources work best for you and your career or business and maintain them over time, but still be willing to modify your selection in the future as your goals change*

15. Brand Development

If you are going to attract the right career or business opportunities from your target audience, they need to able to find you, they need to understand your value and they need to make an exchange.

Building a brand means creating a perception in the marketplace so that every time the person sees that brand, they associate it with the value you offer. It also helps remind anyone else who may know you directly or indirectly about what you do.

As I have discussed previously, sometimes that perception can be affected either positively or negatively, intentionally or unintentionally. There are some aspects of your brand that you can control and some aspects that you cannot control.

If circumstances develop that are beyond your control, you must still be willing to apologize, even if you are not personally at fault. You can apologize for how the person felt if you cannot personally apologize for what happened. For example, a computer system may have generated a problem that has taken hours to rectify. In this case you could say, "I am very sorry for the inconvenience the computer system has caused."

Action 97: *Brand Development involves selecting and implementing the best techniques for reminding people of your value. There are some things you cannot control. You must always be willing to apologize if things go wrong*

15.1 Building Your Personal Brand

If you consistently do what you say you are going to do over time, people start to believe that you are truthful and reliable. If you remember important occasions and reach out to people at these times, you can be remembered very favorably (it is always nice when someone remembers your birthday).

If you have good manners, observe local etiquette and customs and are punctual (in most countries), then over time, you can develop a good personal brand. Don't forget to provide informative feedback when you can (not constructive feedback that is simply thinly disguised criticism) and say thank you as often as possible – and mean it!

In the online world, your personal brand is reflected in the nature of the activity you complete online:

- are you mostly positive or negative?
- do you add value or do you constantly brag, boast or sell?
- do you recognize others?
- do give credit where credit is due?
- do you acknowledge the source of any content you share?
- do you provide value, educate, inform or entertain?
- do you criticize?
- do you ridicule or bully people?
- do you use emoticons?

You may, in certain circumstances, feel perfectly justified and want to retaliate against a negative message, but unfortunately, this only makes you look petty. Take the higher moral ground and remain polite and constructive at all times (but not preachy or paternalistic).

If you would like to establish a personal brand from zero, you may like to associate yourself with a recognized brand. This is how the Beatles rock band got started. Originally, they played songs by other well-known artists and then they started playing their own music. When I was offering a variety of consulting services under my own name, I was not attracting a lot of work. As soon as I started telling people that I specialized in LinkedIn, the work came flooding in.

Action 98: *Understand that everything you do and say both online and offline is part of your personal brand. Always strive to display good manners, etiquette and respect for local customs and say thank you whenever possible*

15.2 Building Your Business Brand

Experts will tell you that there are many aspects to a business brand – and a logo is a very strong visual representation of a business brand. You need to understand how the colors, shape, style and wording appeal (or do not appeal) to your target audience and it is worth making sure that this identity is congruent with your values and purpose.

Many small businesses may have a business brand but the customers and clients associate a person with that brand. When I set up my first online enterprise in 2001, journalists wanted to know about me, not Newcomers Network. I was disappointed, but I soon realized that if you are in your own business, for many people, you are the brand.

Over time, more people have represented Newcomers Network and it has developed into a brand in its own right. That brand has grown across the country and across the world thanks to additional content, events and location representatives. Likewise as a small business grows, the brand replaces the owner and becomes a brand asset in its own right.

The value of the brand is based on the equity that is established – how many people recognize the brand and are aware of what that brand means. What associations do people usually make with that brand? For example, some well recognized car brands want to be known for racing, others for luxury or safety.

A brand can also create a sense of relationship – of belonging to a particular group. It then develops a new level of recognition and in some cases, a level of social capital – think of the brands associated with major sporting teams.

By working on developing a business brand, you have the ability to attract a specific target audience that likes your brand, understands your value, makes a purchase and depending on their experience, keeps coming back for more or recommending it to other like-minded people.

Action 99: *Building a business brand that resonates with your specific target audience is a fantastic business attraction strategy*

15.3 Personal Brand Builders

A good brand drives outcomes. Over time, by building a portfolio of content, customers and conversions, you can be identified as a:

- trusted adviser
- thought leader
- expert
- influencer

- provocateur
- advocate
- missionary
- ambassador
- champion
- guru

These labels take time and energy to earn and are usually bestowed by others (if you call yourself a 'guru' it can appear a bit over the top to others). People generally develop this belief when they see a variety of evidence which could include any or all of the following:

- reputable online content across multiple locations
- journal, magazine and newspaper articles
- regular blog posts
- podcasts and vodcasts
- guest speaking presentations and key note addresses
- e-books or books (published by a publisher or self-published)
- regular and insightful commentary in forums, updates, social media
- media coverage – radio, television, major portals
- significant awards or certifications
- professional memberships (Fellow, Life Member etc)
- officially recognized achievements
- reviews, recommendations, ratings, testimonials
- patents
- significant statistics (saved 10,000 people from an epidemic)

Some people develop a local brand – a great painter or plumber and everyone just knows 'Jack the Plumber' – he doesn't need any formal accolades, just a good word from several people in the local area.

I do not believe that every person needs to establish a comprehensive brand, but I am finding that most people who receive a referral (even about Jack the Plumber) will take a moment and search online for Jack's details. I also know that up to 70% of decision makers will search online for a person before a job interview and 95% will search online before making a final employment decision. People who do not have an online profile run the very real risk of missing out on an opportunity simply because they cannot be 'found' online.

This is why I encourage everyone to at least have a LinkedIn Profile as LinkedIn is highly search engine optimized for names. If you are in your own business, I would also recommend that you create a Google My Business Account under both your name and your business name. This way you can also receive public reviews which add further credibility to your reputation.

Action 100: *There are many different ways to build a personal brand online. Select the most useful for your target audience and one or two that are well recognized (like LinkedIn and Google My Business) to ensure that you appear in internet search results*

15.4 Business Brand Builders

Whilst many of the personal brand builders listed in Section 15.3 can be used for a business brand, in this section I would like to focus more specifically on brand builders that can drive audiences to a business.

- **ratings** – either on your own website or industry aggregators, ratings provide a quick visual representation of your performance. Some ratings are more reliable than others and you will need to find out which ratings are the most coveted in your industry or profession

- **reviews** – can provide a written description about the quality of your goods and services. Some review websites can be sabotaged by competitors or enhanced by business owners. You should try and collect reviews on the best quality review systems, where the reviews process is strictly controlled (as it is with Google Reviews as they monitor the IP address of the poster, they personally read every comment for sales messages or external links, they respond to review complaints etc). You must also personally respond to every review that is received, good or bad, as soon as possible

- **recommendations and testimonials** – similar to personal references, these can be listed on a company website, on a social media platform or on forums or aggregator portals
- **directory listings** – some cities have excellent quality local directories and a listing on one of these directories, especially if it has at least one rating or review, will usually perform very well in internet search results
- **industry specific listings** – there are some industries that have a very united approach towards attracting business and they combine and collaborate and provide summary listings for their industry (for example, individual natural health providers). Many of the individual enterprises may not even have their own website because their listing on the industry list attracts enough business directly (for example, some accommodation providers)

Ultimately, one of the best brand builders is raving fans! People who are more than happy to share the details of your business on a regular basis to their friends, family, networks and your target audience.

Your business can gain additional credibility if this person also happens to be a well-known celebrity (and announces it live in front of the media). You may even choose to pay a well-known identity for some type of endorsement or promotion through their networks (like well-known bloggers or experts) because it attaches your brand to their reputation.

Finally, if you position yourself or your business as the Expert, business will be attracted to you because you are the expert. You don't have to go chasing the target audience, the reputation will attract the target audience.

Action 101: *Ratings, reviews, recommendations, testimonials, directory listings, industry specific listings, fans, celebrities, endorsements and expert status can all attract your target audience to your business*

15.5 Publicity Tactics

Public Relations (PR) people and Agents have been promoting individuals and businesses for a fee for many years. They promise to represent you and secure free promotion through media publicity claiming that they have good relationships with journalists and decision makers. They design campaigns and identify the most likely media outlets that have your target audience.

PR, Communications Experts, Agents and Advisers help create your story for wider distribution. They may coach you on what to say and how to say it. They will not necessarily offer you any guarantee of media coverage but they will often convince you that they are the only people who know how to talk to the media, develop a comprehensive publicity campaign and gain free media coverage.

The irony is that many journalists prefer to talk directly with the 'talent' and not with the 'agent.' You do however run the risk of saying something that could be taken out of context if you are not careful.

Some publicity generated coverage cannot be secured any other way – for example, you cannot buy a 10 minute advertisement during a current affairs television program – but if your business is part of a 10 minute story, how much would that be worth in 'equivalent' advertising dollars?

When choosing potential media outlets for your story, try and match your story with their target audience. If they have a young target demographic and your target demographic is over 45's, then there is a mismatch. However, journalists are sometimes just waiting for a decent story to appear, so if you do have a story that matches their demographic, make sure you send it in and include a call to action.

If your first attempt is not successful, consider sending in another story to the same journalist a month later, then another story, a month later, then another story and so on. Consistency and persistence can work.

Be careful not to make the story all about you or your business as the 'hero.' It is more important to talk about why you are doing something. One of the most successful techniques is the 'problem solving technique.' Alternatively, you may have a human interest story, a topical or seasonal story, a secret to reveal, a solution to a crisis to offer. When you send the story in, don't reveal all of the information, just the bait to catch the fish.

You need to have an incredible headline, a terrific first sentence and your tone needs to be concise and conversational and written in the third person with relevant information accurately quoted. You need to include your contact information and make a call to follow up – but don't mention the word 'publicity' – talk about your 'story.'

This is just a brief overview of some ways to start your publicity journey. It is probably a good idea for you to start with the local newspaper or radio so that you can have some initial practice and ask for feedback. You may also find that they will ask for high resolution photographs, a media kit, further statistics etc and they may be a little more flexible on timing than a live television show screening tonight!

Action 102: *If you would like to secure some free publicity, it is a good idea to start with local publications so that you can build up your experience and resources for the time when a larger media outlet requests information*

16. Network Development

Most people know at least 250 people and feel comfortable with about 150 people in their yearly 'catching up' cycle. This includes family, friends, colleagues, associates, peers, extended connections etc. Thanks to various online tools, some people have thousands of acquaintances. All of these connections are reducing the number of degrees of separation between people – in days gone by, there were usually about six degrees of separation – now, it can be as little as one or two. In other words, I may know one person who knows you even though I have never met you before!

I have been networking for a very long time! My first enterprise, Newcomers Network, was established online in 2001 and of course it is a network. I have learnt a few tricks along the way and I will share them with you now.

Action 103: *The degrees of separation between people are shrinking and thanks to technology, building an extensive network has become easier*

16.1 Assessing Networks

Just as you may wish to develop a career or business, if you are thinking about networking, you need to think about your values and purpose before you start.

When I first started working in real estate (it only lasted a short while although I still have an excellent relationship with my former employer), I went around to all of the local networks to see what they offered and to find out if any of them would be aligned to my role of securing properties for sale. I visited a wide range of different networking groups, most of them more than once.

The once only visits occurred because the groups had a completely different target audience, a completely different value proposition and I did not personally feel any level of synchronicity with either the organizers or the attendees. These were easy to eliminate from my 'future groups list.'

There were some groups that were almost aligned so I suggested that I could be a guest speaker at a future event and share some useful information. These invitations were accepted almost instantaneously and I quickly became known around the area as an expert in social media for real estate (after all, I am an experienced trainer). As the guest speaker, I did not have to worry about introducing myself to other people, I was introduced by the host!

After I completed the speaking circuit (over about three months), I had to decide, given my limited availability, which network or networks I would join and support. I believe that you can only maintain a maximum of three networks on a regular basis.

Unfortunately, none of the networks met enough of my criteria which included:

- target audience reach
- willingness to refer
- spirit of generosity and openness
- friendliness and welcoming attitude towards new arrivals
- reasonable timing schedule (too often or not often enough)
- quality of offering (too formal or too casual)
- consistency and reliability
- reasonable cost (time and expense)

Some of the networks came close, but as I had been networking for years, I made the decision to casually visit some local events so I could keep up my level of knowledge and expertise, but it would be best for me to set up my own network in the local area.

This is not for everyone, but I do often suggest it – if you can't find a network that works for you, create one! However, it is always a good idea to check out the existing networks first and see how they measure up against the assessment criteria above. You may find some networks that are already perfectly aligned and you can secure the knowledge, skills and referrals for your purpose by getting involved. Don't forget that networking involves giving, not just receiving and that 'givers gain.'

Action 104: *Visit a networking group at least twice before joining the group and make sure that they pass your network assessment criteria before you make a regular commitment. Remember that networking involves giving and receiving. If you can't find a network that fits your purpose, consider creating one*

16.2 Creating A Network

If you choose to create a network – be ready for quite a bit of work and be prepared not to get a return in the immediate short term. I have been involved in helping a lot of different networking groups get off the ground and many of the organizers feel as if it is a thankless task. It can be, especially if you go in with unrealistic expectations.

You might start with a very grand idea about hosting exotic events or activities at wonderful venues with amazing guest speakers. When I lived in a smaller city several years ago, it was easy to encourage 100 people to an event. So when I moved to a city three times the size, I automatically assumed I would be able to attract 300 people to an event. I struggled to get 80 people to turn up – and that was after I pulled out every trick in the book – including a very famous and well known sporting identity that cost me $5,000 to speak for just a few minutes. To add insult to injury, one media outlet turned up and asked him about the game on the weekend and nothing about the event he had just spoken at!

What I have also noticed over time (and thanks to technology), is that a lot of people promise to attend but then they do not attend. Free events can have up to 90% of 'no-shows.' If you are an organizer and you have spent a lot of time and money organizing the event, this can be extremely demoralizing.

To distill the process down to what seems to work on an ongoing basis with the least amount of time, money and expense, here is my 'networking group model.'

- give your group a name that is meaningful to your networkers and provide a comprehensive description so that guests know what to expect

- meet on regular basis at a similar time (for example, third Wednesday monthly at 5:30pm) – choose the day and time that will suit most of your target audience networkers but not every networker – that is impossible! For example, mothers with young children may appreciate 10:30am and senior executives may prefer 6:00pm)

- choose a format that does not require too much research, organizing or coordination (finding a perfect unique guest speaker who can confirm months in advance can be difficult nowadays)

- choose a venue that is not normally busy at the time of your event (this way you may be able to secure the venue free of charge or host your event in a particular section whilst other patrons use the main area)

- make a choice about whether there will be an upfront fee or a pay as you go fee (buy your own refreshments). Ironically, some people will not pay $30 up front but will happily spend $30 on refreshments when they get there. Make sure that it is easy for each person to pay for their refreshments independently so that they don't leave early and leave someone else with the bill.

- make sure that you have a system for making everyone feel welcome on arrival – a name tag and an introduction to at least one other person is essential

- encourage everyone to mix throughout the event (if it is a standing event or there is standing time, this makes networking a lot easier)

- break up small groups that congregate exclusively on a regular basis. Part of running a successful network is making sure that it doesn't get stale, so you need a constant flow-through of new networkers at every event. Allow guests who 'don't fit' to pass through and move on to another group

- share the organizing as much as you can – whilst you may be 'required' to be the main conduit, see if you can invite other people to give out the name tags, welcome people on arrival, introduce speakers, request evaluations, say thanks, farewell guests before they leave, follow up after the event, share the event details on social media (before, during and after the event), personally invite people they know to attend etc

- promote the event in a consistent format. This involves using online resources (like Eventbrite or Meetup where people can register), a reminder system (SMS, direct email and social media broadcasts) and personal contact. If possible, send an SMS reminder the day before. Consider adding the event details to other event listings that might be picked up by other publications and always ask people to share the invitation

- take photos and share these on social media (if you have time) and write up a few notes and keep a record of the events on your website etc so that you can maintain some lifetime value from hosting networking events

- personally thank everyone who attended (if you can) – even if just via email or a broadcast on social media
- follow up with any 'free gifts' or resources that you can share, connect with people you meet in relevant forums (like LinkedIn or add them to your database or CRM system)
- work out what worked well and what could be improved and make the next networking event even better

Action 105: *Creating a network requires commitment, but with a good networking group model, you can design a network that will help you achieve your purpose*

16.3 How To Network

It is very tempting to think that if you go out networking, you will be able to 'get' the career or business you desire. However, networking involves both giving and receiving and a few other tricks.

Firstly, before you begin, set your intention. What is your purpose? Who do you want to meet, what do you want to learn and what will the outcome be? What will you provide? How will you choose what events to go to and how will you get there? Can you arrive early and what time do you need to leave? What do you need to bring with you and what will you need to do after the event? What special networking etiquette applies to the event you will be attending?

I have a few simple strategies that you can select for your purpose:

- arrive early so that you are relaxed and don't need to meet too many people at once
- be prepared with your business card or fully charged phone, suitable clothing and mental focus
- be friendly to everyone you meet (including venue staff)
- smile often
- be willing to introduce yourself and invite people on their own to join you or your group
- use people's names in conversation
- ask respectful questions like "How did you find out about this event?" not "And what do you do?"

- be willing to engage in conversation across various topics, not just "let's do business"

- ask for information, not favors – it takes time to build an exchange relationship

- be courteous to others – for example, allow others a turn first before snatching the last cocktail refreshment

- if you make a statement (or a promise) to someone, make sure you follow up and do it, as soon as possible, after the event

- make a point of thanking the host and organizers before leaving

- complete your own follow up after the event – connect to people online, add them to your database, diarize any follow up etc as soon as possible

- reflect on what went well and what could be improved the next time you go networking

- decide whether or not you will book in for the next event of the group and do it

Action 106: *If you plan to network, learn the best tips and techniques for effective networking so that you can attract the right career or business opportunities*

16.4 Developing Your Network

Meeting new people at events and networking is only one part of the process. After the event, you need to decide how you will manage the new relationship in the future. This will again depend upon your purpose.

If you are wanting to attract a specific career, you may want to target particular individuals in a particular industry or profession and then follow up with these people on a regular basis.

If you are in business, you may want to develop very close relationships with key centers of influence and just maintain a presence in the mind of others.

So again, you need to review the concepts of lifetime value and dynamic value. Which people will be added to your core group that you will keep beyond 12 months and which people will you just meet and keep in a more general circle?

If you are extremely clear about your purpose, it will be easy for you to decide who will be on your 'VIP' list (Very Important Person) and who you may never need to see again. It may sound mercenary, but if you are networking on a regular basis, you will need to develop a good system for managing new relationships and maintaining specific relationships.

As soon as I return to my workstation, I make choices. Who will I simply connect to on LinkedIn? Who will I diary to follow up with? Who will I introduce to someone else? Who will I organize to meet again in person? Who will I add to one of my mailing lists? Who will I send something to?

As I am clear on my purpose, I allow various systems to work automatically. By attending some events on a regular basis, some of my key connections automatically see me in person. By publishing content in my newsletters, blog, website and social media, other people are automatically notified about what I am doing. Various algorithms also send updates without me doing anything manually. My diary is used to follow up with VIPs. I send out anything I promised within 24 hours if at all possible.

Likewise, you need to develop your network system for your purpose. As a minimum, I encourage you to keep everyone's details in one place – just 'one source of truth.' It is very difficult to maintain multiple systems. As a general rule, I keep everyone in LinkedIn and have additional lists for various enterprises so that certain people can be kept aligned with individual enterprises (for example, Camberwell Network or Newcomers Network).

Action 107: *Design your own personal system for managing the new people you meet so that you can build your network over time and manage the VIPs for your purpose*

16.5 Valuing Your Network

As I have mentioned, your network will essentially become your 'net-worth.' There is no such thing as job or business security any more. To build a relationship, you need to make at least seven exchanges as a general rule (the quality of your exchanges can also determine how successful the relationship becomes).

I take networking quite seriously. I assume that every person I meet is important and valuable in their own right. I don't look at titles and shuffle myself around to the top CEO. I make an effort to be respectful and polite to everyone I meet.

I overheard a conversation on the train once between two young university graduates who had attended an 'internship information night.' They were discussing how the decision makers were assessing the future potential interns and they both agreed that it went way beyond what each intern was wearing and how they interacted with the decision makers. They observed some candidates who ate or drank too much, who were impolite to other interns or the venue staff, who spoke during speeches, who did not follow standard etiquette by saying please and thank you. They also discussed the suits that people wore, the haircuts, the shoes – I found it very interesting!

Your network can be an incredible source of information and inspiration. A personal phone call to ask a few questions can build rapport. A personal referral or introduction to one of your network members is usually always appreciated. A follow up to a referral you receive is absolutely essential.

If you do not value your network, it will not provide any value to you. If you constantly spam your network with your latest catalogue or special offer, they will tune out from all of your messages. Make an effort to only provide value (either yours or someone else's that you can share) and people will identify you as someone who gives value. Most people normally like to 'repay' the value at some point in the future. Even if they don't, give it anyway.

It is never too early or too late to build your network. I encourage school leavers to start! Networks can be built both online and in person – both networks have value – I would never rely on one or the other.

By valuing your network, you will eventually build and keep loyalty and long term value. You will have people you can trust that you can contact and ask questions. You do not need to be an expert in everything.

A good networker builds long term relationships based on authenticity – and if people perceive you as being completely authentic, even if they don't necessarily agree with everything you do, they remember you, value you and usually provide referrals. You become a magnet to aligned opportunity.

It is also a good idea to realize that your network is not about you, it is about the value you give to others. If they value what you are giving, they will give you opportunities.

Action 108: *By valuing your network and the relationships with your network members, you will become a magnet for the right career and business opportunities*

17. Website Development

My first website went online in 2001 and wow, websites have changed a lot since then. Some of the principles that applied then still apply today. You have to be clear about your purpose before you begin. You need to work with professionals and you need to realize that it will constantly need to be updated, it will never be finished. It also needs to transform over time as careers and businesses transform. Websites may have started as a publishing vehicle, now they are becoming an exchange vehicle. Who knows, perhaps in the future they will be part of our body!

Action 109: *Remember that a website is never finished and must constantly be updated and evolved over time*

17.1 Personal Career Attraction Website

If you have chosen to have a website to attract a career position, there are a number of choices to make. Firstly, I will assume that you know what type of position you are seeking, both now and in the future. You then need to think about:

- will I use a free blog or website platform first and upgrade later?
- will I use my own name for the domain name or the topic name of what I want to be known for? (I recommend the first option)
- will I pay for my own website hosting and my own domain name through two different companies (for greater transferability in the future) and then have a website set up (either by me or an expert) or will I ask a website designer to host and create my website for me (not recommended)?
- will I create a site map before I start building the website with some basic elements and structure or will I just get started and play around as I go? (I recommend the first option)
- will I get some advice on the design, colors, layout, styling etc first?
- will I start thinking about how I can use the website in the future?

Building a website just so that you can attract a career position may seem a little overwhelming, particularly if you are not technologically savvy. Fortunately nowadays there are many free or low-cost solutions. If you want a free option and most of your content will be text, not video, I would suggest that you start with WordPress.com http://wordpress.com as this can be exported later (to WordPress.org) and the basic version is free of charge and your account will never be deleted (so you can be immortal!).

If you can purchase your own domain name through a separate domain name registration company, that is preferable. Then, when you login to your WordPress.com account, for a small yearly fee, you can 'map' your WordPress.com website to your domain name so it will appear at the domain name address – for example http://sueellson.com instead of http://sueellson.wordpress.com

I choose to pay for my own website hosting and have created my websites using WordPress.org as my website design platform. I have chosen website hosting that allows me to have more than one website and more than one email address. I believe it is more professional to have an email address like sueellson@sueellson.com than sueellson@gmail.com (although I do recommend using a Gmail type account as the Administration contact just in case the website hosting crashes and I cannot access my webserver email).

I use Bluehost.com for my website hosting and this is an affiliate link https://www.bluehost.com/track/sueellson/ (if you choose to use this link, I may receive a referral fee but I will not have access to your details).

The content on your personal career attraction website will depend on your purpose. You may want to provide a biography and a career summary, a photo and a portfolio of non-commercially sensitive information. You may like to describe the type of work you would like to do and showcase some of your thoughts in a blog section. You may like to curate a variety of content to show that you really do understand your industry or profession.

If you go down this path, I also recommend that you:

- set up a Google Plus account http://plus.google.com and in the Links section, link to your personal career attraction website address and any other content that appears online that has your details in it

- set up a LinkedIn account http://linkedin.com and add in a link to your personal career attraction website address in the Contact Information part in the 'Websites' section by choosing 'Other' and then adding in the name of your website and the link
- add the personal career attraction website address to your email signature, business card, resume, CV etc

Depending on the nature of your industry or profession, you may also have an online profile on an industry specific portfolio website. Whilst that may be helpful in the industry, just remember that your own website has lifetime value.

If setting up your own personal career attraction website is too much at this point, please complete a LinkedIn Profile as this will rank particularly well in search engine results and it will give you a framework for collecting information that you could add to your personal career attraction website in the future (it is also a fantastic starting point).

Action 110: *A personal career attraction website provides a lifetime value record of your career and allows you to attract future career opportunities. You can choose a free WordPress.com site that can be exported at a later date or start with your own domain name website with personally purchased website hosting and WordPress.org as your website design platform*

17.2 Personal Business Attraction Website

As discussed in 17.1, all of the same principles apply. In this case, instead of attracting a career opportunity, you would like to attract a business opportunity.

That business opportunity could be related to some sort of products or services.

If you are just starting out as a consultant, you may like to do some internet research on 'Authority Websites' – this is where you set up a website in either your own name or the name of your consultancy and the information you provide convinces the search engines and the person visiting your website that you are worth hiring. You would need to include information like:

- description of your services (you choose whether or not to include your fees)
- your past results and achievements (non-commercially sensitive)
- possibly a list of clients (if non-commercially sensitive)
- some ratings, reviews or testimonials
- some information for the media
- calls to action and contact details
- special accreditations, certifications, memberships, big trusted brand names associated with you

Alternatively, if you want to start offering services but you don't want to have your own website, you could list your offerings on a freelancer portal (for example Fiverr, Upwork, Freelancer etc)

If you are selling products, you would need to have an appropriate selling platform or e-commerce solution included although some people start with a separate website and then sell through a different shopping service (for example, eBay, Etsy, Amazon, Alibaba etc), particularly if they want to test the market before having the full website development costs from day one. Some people also choose the shopping service option first because they know that the shopping service already has an engaged audience of interested buyers.

If people come to your website and it does not meet their needs quickly, you will probably lose the sale. Whilst you may want to sell to them the first time they visit your website, some businesses have become very successful at attracting multiple visits before the first sale (for example, they have a really informative blog and then one day, after multiple visits, the person buys the products or services – this is a very good strategy for high end products).

Action 111: *A personal business attraction website allows you to attract business career opportunities directly. When you start, you can either use it as a one stop shop or in conjunction with a freelancer portal or shopping service*

17.3 General Website Attraction Techniques

There are some general priorities I recommend for every website that is published:

- make sure you have a comprehensive list of primary and secondary keywords that you are trying to optimize across your entire website and incorporate these appropriately in all of your current content and future content on your website and other online content that is published elsewhere
- create a Google Account and install Google Analytics, register with Google Search Console and set up Google Alerts for your name and your business name
- make sure your website is 'mobile-friendly' – this is also called 'responsive' design – Google will penalize you if your website is not suitable for mobile devices
- make sure you have backup, security, search engine optimization and caching features installed (with WordPress.org, there are plugins that provide these features)
- choose a website design that loads quickly (a caching plugin can help)
- add quality content on a regular basis
- connect the relevant social media profiles to your website and broadcast your new website content via your social media channels
- add your website to other directory listings in your local area, in your industry and profession

It is also a good idea to keep an eye on your competitors. Find out what keywords they are optimizing (right click your mouse on a blank area of their website and choose 'View page source' so that you can see the source code that has been used to create the website). Somewhere on the screen, you will be able to see the page title, keywords and description and this will include the keywords (if they have been set) for the website.

By looking at your competitors and colleagues, you can refine your own offering.

For example, one of my course participants offered art therapy classes. Unfortunately, many local aged care facilities had stopped hiring qualified art therapy professionals because they found that art therapy students could offer a similar service for 'free' because they were looking for work experience. My participant already knew this, so she was a bit apprehensive about spending money on her own website.

When she did a competitor analysis before setting up her own website, she found another art therapist who was offering 'art therapy supervision services.' This woman was completely booked out, so my course participant realized that if she set up an 'art therapy supervision' service on her website (which she was also qualified to do), then she would still be able to work in her field. She would never have realized this if she had not looked at other like-minded businesses.

This same course participant also taught yoga. When she looked at most of the other yoga teacher websites, she found that most of them were all using the same stock photos. She quickly realized that her website would be much more interesting to visitors if she used her own photos. Another benefit of doing her own competitor analysis research.

Action 112: *Every website that is published should be connected to Google, have backup, security, caching and SEO features installed, load quickly, be mobile friendly, have new content added regularly, be connected to social media and be added to relevant directory listings*

17.4 Website Performance Measures

If you are generating exactly the type of career or business opportunities you would like, then you know that your website is working well. In fact, I don't worry too much about minute specifics if the work keeps flowing.

That said, I know that major corporations will spend hours analyzing their data analytics information and they will work out how to increase conversions by 2% if they move a screen button to a different spot or change the color! If you are talking about a million dollars of turnover per day, this can make a huge difference to the bottom line.

For an average individual or small enterprise, here are some general targets to aim for:

- site speed – make sure each page of your website loads in less than four seconds
- bounce rate – less than 55% (you want to encourage people to visit more than one page of your website before they bounce off and go to another website)
- time on your website – more than two minutes
- pages per visit – more than two pages

If you can achieve these results, you will be doing very well. You may also like to track and monitor:

- most common sources of traffic (organic, paid, direct, other links)
- percentage of people visiting via a mobile device
- overall daily or monthly statistics (static or upward trend)
- referrals from social media
- most common entry pages
- most common exit pages

This information will give you some clues as to how well your website is performing and help you understand what is worth investigating and improving. As a minimum, I believe it is important for you to understand these variables and how your choices will affect these results. These results can all be seen very easily through your Google Analytics account and your website designer should give you full access to this information (ideally, you would create the Google Analytics account and then give the website designer access to it – that way, if you want to stop working with that website designer, you can delete them from your account).

An expert can give you much more detailed analysis and do split A/B testing, generate specific customized reports, track eye movements and user behavior, provide keyword analysis and a whole lot more.

Action 113: *Make sure that you understand the basic performance measures of your website and how to see these results via your Google Analytics account*

17.5 User Experience And Website Feedback

When I first started learning about creating a website, every website designer was talking about 'usability.' Over time, the terminology has changed, user experience, UX, customer experience, CX, traffic, conversions etc

Regardless of what terminology is used, every website owner needs to understand how the website suits (or doesn't suit) the target audience. You may love your website, but if it is not attracting the target audience and converting into the career or business opportunities you seek, then it is time to review your website.

You might like to start by asking various people you know, of different ages and backgrounds, what they think of your website and what are their general impressions and thoughts. Do not justify any of your reasons as to why it is the way it is. Just ask them to talk you through what they are doing and thinking as they interact with your website. Make notes, not judgments. You may find some good surprises and some bad surprises – but do not act at this point. Seek additional clarification if needed.

Make sure you also try and find someone who is part of your target audience and see if you can spend a few moments with them and see how they interact with your website. Make some more notes, again, no judgments.

Now it is time to collate all of the comments and suggestions and sit down with your business advisor, key staff and website designer and discuss the findings. You may agree to make small changes in the short term and plan bigger changes in the future. You may decide that you need a complete overhaul. Again, don't forget to review what your competitors are doing before you make any final decisions.

Also, before you make a major change, make sure you know very specifically what is working well for you. It would be ridiculous to make a significant change based on one person's experience if that affected 95% of your other users and created a decline in conversions.

Taking ownership is a key component of this process. Try not to be overruled by someone who is technologically more competent. They do not have the same level of personal investment in your website (or business) and they could easily make a suggestion that may work for a different target audience but you know that it will not work for your target audience.

Let me share an example. If you are a trade website, you know that your audience already understands all of the terminology and doesn't want copious amounts of text describing everything in minute detail multiple times. They want to quickly login and complete their transactions. A slow performing website and a difficult to order process could see them quickly move to another provider. In this case, the efficiency of the process could be more important than extra keywords.

Most users also expect some basics. Google expects to see an 'About Us' page and a 'Contact Us' page. I always have a 'Site Map' page so that if someone wants to see everything at once, they can. I follow a very strict style guide too – making every effort to keep my formatting similar throughout my website. Understanding your minimum requirements is important so that you can direct the website designer rather than the website designer direct you. In my view, the best website designers work in collaboration with you.

Action 114: *Seek input from other people and your target audience about how your website works from their perspective and then consider making changes in conjunction with your website designer*

18. Overcoming Challenges

Throughout the book, I have mentioned some challenges that you may have to overcome. Your own inner critic. The reasons you have been given when you missed out on an opportunity. Procrastination.

You have probably heard how cigarette smokers have woken up one day and decided, I am not going to smoke ever again and they never do. However, this is very rare. Most people take multiple attempts to finally give up smoking.

So it is with challenges. No sooner do we recover from one challenge, we then find another appears. Sometimes the challenges get easier, other times they get harder. Sometimes we learn the wrong way to deal with a situation, other times, we handle things really well because we have either learnt from our past mistakes or we have learnt specific skills so that we could cope when the challenge arrived (I certainly encourage every parent to learn parenting skills – it doesn't solve all of the issues but it certainly helps!)

If you are constantly missing out on the career or business opportunities you are seeking or you are not attracting the career or business opportunities you would like, please consider the following:

- do your target audience really understand your value?
- are you self-sabotaging in any way (with negative thoughts or hidden worries)?
- are limiting beliefs holding you back and stopping you from taking the action you need to take?
- are you using time tested systems that work or doing ad hoc things casually?
- are you eating well, exercising and looking after your health?
- are you surrounding yourself with people who can encourage you and support you?
- are you stuck with recurring thoughts as to why you have missed out rather than moving forward with proactive action steps?

- are you listening to the feedback you receive and analyzing the data from your research to improve your career or business attraction strategies?
- are you doing your best to make sure that you are in the right place at the right time as often as possible (both online and in person)?

When a new client comes to me with a grand plan to change their life, we sit down and work out what needs to happen over the next six months to two years. There are a lot of action steps that can be completed immediately and these usually generate a significant mind shift and some short term results.

The most proactive clients usually achieve exactly what they want within six months, because they are completely committed to taking action. They get up when they are knocked down. They find new ways and better ways all the time. They ask for help. They get encouragement. They feel inspired. They focus. And they don't stop.

If you want to change your life and the direction of your future, you will need to overcome challenges. You will need to be persistent and sometimes patient (I personally find it very hard to be patient!).

What I can assure you is that if you keep up your momentum and keep taking action, even if it takes a full two years to reach your first desired destination, at the two year mark, you will be able to look back and celebrate everything you have done to achieve your goal. You may only be 50% of the way to your second desired destination but if you hadn't done anything, you would still be back at your original location.

Don't live with the pain of regret. Overcome your challenges. Be resilient. Be persistent. Achieve your goals.

Action 115: *On your journey to attracting the right career or business opportunities, you will face challenges. Don't stop. Keep taking action and be persistent and when you look back, you will see how far you have come*

18.1 Action Planning Sequence

Mapping out what you plan to do to attract the right career or business opportunities could seem a little overwhelming. As you have been reading this book, I hope that you have been making notes about which options you would like to try in the future. Now it is time to sort them into a logical order!

Firstly, make sure you have written them all down. I encourage you to start off with some quick wins. Tasks that are quick and easy to complete and don't require a huge investment of money. I also encourage you to start collecting all of the information you are going to need – passwords, logins, records, reports, resumes, photos etc

The second set of tasks to complete are the activities that will require a beginning, a middle and an end. In other words, before the task is fully completed, several steps, that may take time, have to be completed. It may be important with these tasks to initiate a process but then wait before the next step is completed – for example, apply for membership of a Professional Association. I encourage you to do this early on in the timeline so that whilst you are in the 'waiting' stage, you can complete other tasks.

The third priority is to set up quality real estate everywhere. Sort out your own records, update your resume or CV, complete your selected online and offline profiles, update your usernames and passwords list, commission a new profile photo or business logo, make sure your business descriptions are consistent and relevant for your target audience and include your keywords and links etc.

You now have your foundations in place. If you are really proactive, you may have also started decluttering your house, your pantry (of foods you know you shouldn't be eating) and your garage or storage facility.

On the path to your new future, you do not need to keep absolutely everything from your past. You might also like to make regular sleep and exercise a priority in your life and reduce your amount of screen time so that you have a genuine opportunity to relax and unwind and spend quality time with your loved ones.

So far, you may not have spent too much time sourcing professional assistance, but now you really need to move into the research phase. To examine what worked well for the thought leaders, experts, peers, mentors, leaders etc in your career or business field. You need to review your options and start dipping your toe in the water and trying a few things – implementing some of your attraction strategies and monitoring the results. You may like to set up a schedule of what you plan to do on what days of the week so it is manageable and you need to do this for at least three months.

At the end of the three months, you need to review your results. What is working well, what could be improved, what else could you try? Create a plan for your next three months. Again, keep records of what is happening along the way – record the wins and the losses because it is so easy to forget the wins and it can be painful if you only focus on the losses.

Six months have now passed, so it is time to review the entire process. Look at your original goals. How are you going? What has been wonderful? What hasn't worked well? Most importantly, what do you need to focus on next? What action steps do you need to take? What additional support or encouragement do you need? What must you let go of or say no to? What is your next goal?

Action 116: *Planning the various actions that you will complete in date order with realistic time frames will help you achieve your goals. Remember to review what works and keep a record of your wins and losses so that you can celebrate your achievements and plan your next action steps*

18.2 Measuring Results

I have mentioned several times how important it is to measure your results on your career and business attraction journey. There are various ways to do this:

- compile a comprehensive list of your usernames and passwords with the date that you started each record (you can see how the list grows over time)

- a spreadsheet of real time statistics that you collect from your online profiles – Connections, Views, Likes etc (to track your growth)

- an action plan with tasks allocated by date and a way to recognize when the tasks have been completed or rescheduled (so you can see how much you have done)

- a record of your wins and the outcomes (so you can celebrate)

- a record of things that didn't go well and the actions you chose to take afterwards (so you don't repeat a mistake)

- ongoing records of the useful findings you have collected from your research (so that you can review your previous findings or re-use the strategies as required)
- a record of dates – when you changed to a role that was more aligned or you sourced a significant number of target audience clients and made more sales

You may have other internal or external, formal or informal systems for tracking your progress:

- number of career invitations, job applications or interviews
- new clients, sales, testimonials, reviews
- increase in salary or profits
- increase in scalability or asset value
- improved sleep, exercise and health standards
- reduction in clutter and chaos
- increase in completed actions and patience

Every step in the right direction will be one step closer to attracting the right career or business opportunity. You are signaling that you are ready and prepared to do what it takes. Every journey allows you to take a short rest on the way – but if you want to reach the destination, you cannot stop. You need to keep going until you get there.

Action 117: *By measuring your results along your career or business attraction journey, you will see how the actions you are taking are helping you reach your destination. Don't stop. Keep going*

18.3 Personal Blockages

At the beginning of this section, I listed some general questions to ask yourself about why you may or may not be achieving success when looking at attracting the right career or business into your life.

In this section, I would like to identify some of the common 'reasons' that I hear.

- **I am not successful because 'insert limiting belief'**

Did you know that repeatedly saying something to yourself will eventually make you believe it? I am too old, too young, too experienced, not experienced enough etc. Negative affirmations can be very destructive. Try changing over to a positive affirmation – I am wise, I have plenty of time ahead of me, I have valuable gifts to share, I am willing to learn – see how much more attractive these are to a positive outcome?

- **I have applied for over 100 jobs and haven't got one interview**

If I did something 100 times and I didn't get a result, I would change what I was doing! If something isn't working after 10 times, change it. Find a better way to do things. Get some advice.

- **I have had a bad past – everything has gone wrong, nothing works etc**

Every day you have a choice. To either repeat a version of yesterday or do some of what you did yesterday and something new today. What one little thing could you do today that is different to what you did yesterday? Drink an extra glass of water to help your body function a little better? Go for a five minute walk? Pat a dog or a cat? Talk to someone you haven't talked to in a while? Listen to some positive music? All of these things are free.

If you start doing just one thing different today, you will soon be tempted to do something else a little different tomorrow. Over the course of a year, you may find that you have done more than 50 different things to what you did in the previous year – what an improvement! You will definitely attract better outcomes.

- **I simply don't have the energy or the motivation to change**

Are you happy with where you are now? What is the cost to you if you do not change?

What you have done up until this point has created some of your circumstances. What you can do will create other circumstances. You don't have to change everything at once (that would be way too challenging). Remember that it is never too late (even if the absolute worst thing ever has already happened). No time is wasted. Smile – and start.

Stop asking yourself Why? That gives you an opportunity to create an excuse.

As yourself How? Or What? That gives you an opportunity to create and complete an action.

Action 118: *Think about what personal blockages you might be carrying with you right now and think about one thing you could do today that is slightly different from yesterday. See if you can repeat it tomorrow as well and have a look in a year's time and see what is different about your life*

18.4 External Blockages

I am not completely naïve. I know full well that there some direct external blockages that can be difficult to overcome – some external influences that you cannot change. What you can change is how you respond to them.

- **The career opportunities I am looking for just don't exist anymore**

Perhaps the industry you have been working in for many years is slowly disappearing. Over the last 100 years, there have been many different industries that have simply died and been replaced by either technology or cheaper labor in another country. That doesn't mean you must be unemployed.

What it does mean is that you need to look very closely at your transferable skills. In every job, there are skills that can be applied to another job. You also need to think about some of your other interests, because you could re-train in another field and start a whole new career that is perhaps even more aligned with your interests.

For example, I was working with a very nice young man who had moved to a new country and he had an extensive background in international textile purchasing. After months of focused career searching, he realized that there were very few jobs in this industry in his new country and that the roles that did exist were usually filled by locals who had been in the industry for many years. He had such a lovely personable manner and whilst he was looking for work, he had a part time voluntary job helping new migrants and another part time job to pay the bills. He had always been interested in helping people, so he eventually decided to stop looking for work in textiles and he has enrolled in a social work course. Whilst it wasn't his first choice for a career when he moved to the new country, he is now extremely excited about his studies and his new career because he has always liked talking to people (and he has a great smile and a very warm heart!).

- **There are unconscious biases in the minds of decision makers**

Unfortunately, regardless of how many affirmative action programs that are implemented, or diversity training programs run or even public awareness campaigns shared, there will always be decision makers who refuse to consider you for a particular role. This is extremely annoying and unfortunately, the best you can do in this case is just accept it and move on. Consistency and persistency will always triumph.

- **Market forces are driving away opportunities in certain areas or reducing rewards for the same work**

Many years ago, I was able to secure training work for a substantial fee per day. Now, I am lucky to secure a few hours at a time for a very low hourly rate. At the same time, I am still paying 99 cents per kilogram for bananas despite the fact that more than 10 years have passed (I have already mentioned that I like going to that cheap green grocer shop!).

Yes, some work benefits have definitely gone down, other lifestyle benefits have gone up. We all tend to have a selective memory and think back to a time when one isolated item was cheaper. Yes, the price of housing has gone up, but the cost of interest has gone down and we now expect a bigger house than we did before.

I firmly believe that if you budget carefully, regardless of where you live in the western world, you have the ability to maintain a modest lifestyle (even if that involves sharing your accommodation). I understand that it is not always ideal, but sometimes, living within our means makes life so much simpler. Rather than try and live according to the standards set by other people or the media, be grateful for what you do have and see how much more is automatically attracted to you. If you complain about what you don't have and you will never have enough.

Action 119: *Understand that sometimes in life, you cannot change the external environment, you can only adapt to the external environment. Find out what you can re-use, how you can maintain your consistency and persistence and be extremely grateful for everything you have right now*

18.5 Top 20 Tips And Techniques

After reading through the book (or skipping to this section), I would like to share my top 20 tips and techniques for attracting the right career or business into your life.

1. Start with understanding your highest value and purpose and use this as a tool for selecting the actions you will take to attract the right career or business opportunities.

2. Once you have chosen your highest value and purpose, clarify your vision of the future and identify the people, processes and possibilities that you can utilize to help you achieve your goals.

3. On your journey, watch out for the underlying needs, limiting beliefs, anecdotal information and influence of others that could affect your choices and actions.

4. Success is built on taking regular action in alignment with your values. You may need to be in an alternative career or business for a short time to enable you to ultimately achieve your purpose in the long term.

5. Develop a capital raising mindset and find ways to increase your social, intellectual, cultural, financial, gratitude, operating, relationship, credibility and influence capital on your journey.

6. Accept full responsibility for completing the best actions for your purpose. Start by doing one new thing today.

7. Create a quality online and offline profile so that the decision makers or target audiences that need to find you can find you.

8. To build your attraction power, you will need to build lifetime value and dynamic value. Lifetime value will help you create an asset to build upon, dynamic value will allow you to remain relevant and current in your environment.

9. As you implement your actions, collect the results, analyze and improve your ongoing strategic activities and consider 'pay to play' and professional assistance options.

10. Remember to always provide positive feedback, say thank you whenever you can, follow up after every interaction and smile, even when you are concentrating!

11. Securing the right career or business opportunity is about aligning your value with the career or business opportunity. This involves finding the right fit and saying 'no' to the wrong opportunity and saying 'yes' if it is outside of your comfort zone but aligned with your values and purpose.

12. Attraction involves identifying and implementing multiple concurrent strategies across multiple channels and media. You will need to be persistent and consistent.

13. Every target audience (for a career or a business opportunity), expects to have a personalized experience that matches their needs. Understand what information you need to provide and what format they expect and make sure you deliver it.

14. Attraction is also based on an exchange of value. Increase your level of real, perceived, referral, clarity, reciprocity, uncertainty, pricing, human, asset and investment value and you will attract more value.

15. Target audiences, once identified, can be contacted, aroused and attracted. If you attract people from outside your target audience range, consider how you can adjust your attraction techniques so that you can be more efficient and effective.

16. Content is a key attraction technique in the digital era. You need to find ways to create, curate and share content in a way that leads to conversions.

17. People can provide you with the help, ideas, inspiration and motivation to complete your attraction actions. Aim to build trust, loyalty and credibility and always find ways to improve your own personal standards.

18. Platforms provide a range of automatic and manual tools to help you attract career and business opportunities. They are constantly changing, so make sure you adopt a lifelong learner approach so that you can maximize their value.

19. The right processes and possibilities will ultimately lead to a quality personal or business brand that can continue to attract career and business opportunities. Find out what will work for your values and purpose and do it. Find ways to overcome the challenges on your journey and celebrate your achievements.

20. Ultimately your success depends on the quality of the real and virtual networks you build around you. LinkedIn allows you to build and develop the people network and your own website allows you to create a personal or business archive network, so consider both of these as key components of your ongoing attraction success.

Action 120: *Review the Top 20 Tips and Techniques and make an effort to complete at least one of these in the next month*

19. Full List Of 120 Actions

Introduction

Action 1: Think about your life as it is right now and make a note of what you are most grateful for and what is working well. Also write down one thing that you would like to do differently after reading this book.

Action 2: Part of attracting the right career and business opportunities into your life is realizing that you must be fully aware of your highest values before you begin. What is your highest value right now?

Action 3: If you are clear about your purpose, you will be able to make the right choices. Take steps to increase your overall level of clarity – don't wait until a crisis occurs. On a scale of 1 to 10 with 10 being the most clear and 1 being the least clear, what number would you give your current level of clarity today? Write down the number and the date.

Action 4: Look at your life so far and write down the names of the three most significant people in it. Next to each person's name, write down the most valuable experience each person has given you, whether or not it was aligned with your values, purpose or future goals and see how that has shaped the choices you have made up to this point.

Section 1. It's All About You

Action 5: Write down three beliefs that you have about yourself that are not serving you well. Think about what happened at the time you created those beliefs and re-assess whether or not they are 'true' beliefs or 'circumstantial' beliefs. Now is the time to let go of limiting beliefs and start creating potential beliefs.

Action 6: Accept full responsibility for all of your actions and always operate on the basis of a fair exchange – pay for a benefit you receive and reward the creator so that you in turn can be rewarded for your efforts.

Action 7: Identify the three best ways to make sure you complete the actions you choose to do in the future, remembering that unless you have absolute clarity, your chances of conversion will be limited.

Action 8: Be prepared to learn new skills through formal and informal training for the rest of your life. Don't be worried about making mistakes, especially if you are taking calculated risks – just keep taking action.

Action 9: Selecting and completing a variety of actions that are both easy and challenging will lead you to results. Find people and services that can help you on your journey.

Section 2. Past and Present Context

Action 10: Allocate up to 10% of your time to constantly learn, grow and develop to remain employable both now and in the future.

Action 11: Ask yourself how you will set the framework for your future decision making in an uncertain environment. Decide whether or not you need some coaching assistance to create your personal model for the future.

Action 12: Write down three things you could realistically achieve in the next three months. Visualize yourself after you have completed each of these tasks. Imagine the smile on your face, the feeling inside your body and where you will be. Make it feel as real as possible and then write down how you will celebrate each of those achievements.

Action 13: Write down one thing that you need to let go of to move forward in your life. Be as descriptive as possible – what, how, when, where, why and with who it happened. Then work out what type of professional could help you let go of this issue. Find this professional and make an appointment to see them.

Action 14: Write down the number one thing in your life that you value more than anything else. Describe the value that it gives you and how it adds meaning and purpose to your life.

Action 15: Look at your life right now and identify any subconscious needs that could be interfering with your values and your ability to align your actions with your purpose. Write them down and work out how you will get these needs met so that you can move towards your true values and purpose.

Action 16: Write down the names of at least two people who have believed in you. Write down what they believed about you and how that has inspired you on your journey so far. Consider contacting at least one person you know and telling them about your beliefs in their abilities.

Action 17: If you are going to attract the right career or business for your purpose, look at yourself in relation to the other people around you and how they are influencing your choices. If necessary, establish new boundaries so that you can make better decisions in the future.

Section 3. Selecting The Right Career Or Business

Action 18: Either go through the Mind Map Process to define your future career or business or record it so that all of your future actions are in alignment with your future direction.

Section 4. Choosing What To Do Right Now

Action 19: Rather than choosing what to do at any point in time, start choosing what is best to do as a starting point. If you want to move to a new career or business, you need to showcase the value that is of most interest to the decision maker.

Action 20: Write down two of the worst decisions you have made in your life and why they were bad decisions. Then write down what you could have done at the time to make a better decision so that you can make better decisions in the future. Remember that one decision does not have the power to rule you for life.

Section 5. Capital Raising

Action 21: Develop a capital raising mindset so that you can attract the right career and business opportunities.

Action 22: Choose the most relevant voluntary activities to complete on a regular basis so that you can develop a true sense of belonging and increase your social capital.

Action 23: Choose the most relevant formal and informal education to complete in the future so that you can continue to develop your personal intellectual capital.

Action 24: Find out how you can increase your cultural capital (or cultural exposure) so that you can receive greater insights and opportunities beyond your standard frame of reference.

Action 25: Have a realistic look at how you have managed your financial capital in the past and decide whether or not you need to make any changes so that you will be in a position to attract the right career or business that is aligned with your true values in the future.

Action 26: Write down three things you are most grateful for in your life right now. Consider how these three things have led to your current level of success and enable you to keep going or can help you attract the right career or business in the future.

Action 27: Reflect on the most important people in your life right now and the people who are your highest priority. Are they helping or hindering your progression? Write down three things you could to improve your relationship capital.

Action 28: Reflect on the people and businesses you know that you believe are highly credible. What do these people do and say that helps you believe that they are credible? What could you do to be more credible?

Action 29: By increasing the standards of your own behavior, you will influence your own outcomes and the effect your behavior has on the people around you. Increasing your influence capital will increase the number of career and business opportunities that appear in your life.

Section 6. Action Steps

Action 30: Suggestions will only be helpful to you if you accept responsibility for completing the associated actions.

Action 31: Complete the necessary qualitative and quantitative research associated with your chosen career or business, assess this detail, select the places where you will share this information and then collect the information you need to add to the various online and offline platforms.

Action 32: Based on your very clear purpose and the most effective online and offline platforms for attracting the right decision makers for your career or business, complete your selected profiles in an accurate, reliable and consistent format.

Action 33: After completing your online and offline profiles, revisit each profile and add in more details and then ask a variety of people to review your details so that you can tweak it even further based on your research and purpose.

Action 34: Select a range of life time and real time activities that you can complete (or outsource) on a manageable and regular basis so that you can maximize your attraction power. Gaining preliminary ownership level knowledge and then hiring a professional on an individual basis will be quicker and more effective than trying to do everything yourself.

Action 35: After using various platforms for at least three months, review and analyze the performance and results. Find ways to improve your efficiency and effectiveness. Also consider 'pay to play' options.

Action 36: Find ways every day to give descriptive feedback, follow up with people you already know, say thank you and smile. It will change your life for the better!

Action 37: Remember to celebrate victories, acknowledge achievements and learn what does and doesn't work. Do this for yourself and for others.

Action 38: After completing each action step cycle, pause and make some decisions on what you will do next so that you can continue to attract the right career or business opportunities.

Section 7. Career Attraction Tips And Techniques

Action 39: To attract the right career, you need to be able to showcase your skills, knowledge, networks and attitude in a location where the right decision makers can find it. Your greatest need is someone else's opportunity.

Action 40: If you need an immediate job right now, remember that you need to have the right attitude, excellent job search skills, accurate information and the ability to effectively showcase your value before and during the job interview.

Action 41: Identify the real value you are receiving from a survival or means to an end job and develop your job search skills and career attraction strategies so that your next job is more closely aligned to your values.

Action 42: Be willing to say 'no' to the wrong opportunity and 'yes' to the right opportunity, even if you have to overcome an immediate benefit or potentially difficult challenges in the future. Make a conscious choice aligned with your values.

Action 43: When considering your 'next step up job,' look very carefully at the information you have gathered about the role and the organization and be discerning in the selection process. It needs to be an aligned fit and you need to assess multiple variables before accepting the role.

Action 44: Select the five main job identification methods you believe will be most effective for finding the job you would like and review any others that may complement your selection. Actively use them.

Action 45: If you provide a tailor made job application for each job you apply for, you are much more likely to attract the right opportunity. You also need to make sure that your application is screen friendly.

Action 46: If you are truly genuine in your desire to attract the right job opportunity, you will need to be extremely persistent and there are many tasks that you will need to complete. Be courageous and keep going!

Action 47: Learn the basic principles of job interviews and learn new skills from each job interview that you attend. See every interview as an opportunity to learn and grow and one step closer to your job goal.

Action 48: Follow up after every job interview and always make sure that you include a message of thanks and a call to action for the future.

Action 49: Make sure that you receive your job offer in writing and give yourself time to review the offer, make a decision and complete any administration. Once accepted, make sure that you are fully prepared to start the new role on day one.

Section 8. Business Attraction Tips and Techniques

Action 50: Business provides a value exchange and to attract more business, provide more value.

Action 51: Before you invest in a business (either a start-up or an existing business), assess the real value that the products or services provide to customers and make sure that there is a sustainable market of potential customers that you can attract. Be aware of basic business sustainability principles.

Action 52: Business owners need to understand how they can influence the perceived value in their products and services and how they will manage the situation if a bad perception is created.

Action 53: Businesses need to choose the best ways to continually attract referrals to their business by making sure that there is an interest in the product or service, a group of people who can easily find and verify the product or service and then feel comfortable paying the set price. The methodology for sourcing these referrals will continue to change over time.

Action 54: Whether you are about to start a business or continue in an existing business, make sure that you are very clear about why you are in business, how you will do it and who you will serve – this clarity will attract opportunity, confusion will drive customers away.

Action 55: Although it may be uncomfortable at first, be willing to share business opportunities on a reciprocal basis as it can be a great tool for increasing your ability to attract new business opportunities.

Action 56: Be willing to make decisions in an uncertain environment. Develop your own decision making strategy and find ways to cope with consequences. Remember that even the worst situations have hidden blessings.

Action 57: Look at your business and who you exchange value with and look at ways to identify the total value that you share. Calculate any payment exchanges based on the value of your exchange rather than simply the time and costs of your exchange.

Action 58: Every person associated with a business is expecting more now than they have in the past. The businesses and the people that will attract the best opportunities are the people who are willing to constantly learn, grow and adapt to the changing environment.

Action 59: Build the fixed, current and digital assets of your business so that you can continue to attract the right type of business and build the asset value of the business. If you do this, when it is time to sell the business, you will receive a good return on your investment of time, money and energy.

Action 60: Every business owner needs to think like an investor and collect the information that an investor would need to assess the value of your business. This will help you attract an investor or a good sale price in the future.

Section 9. Audience Attraction Techniques

Action 61: Carefully defining your target audience will allow you to calculate where they congregate so that you can select the best methods for attracting them to you for a career or business.

Action 62: Before choosing the most appropriate target audience locations, test and assess their ability to convince your target audience of your value offering. Make sure that what you do offer is clearly visible to the target audience (without being forceful) so that they can select you for the right career or business opportunity.

Action 63: Helping your target audience understand what you have to offer as a career or business in a timely, effective and informative way will significantly increase your ability to attract the right career or business.

Action 64: Having the courage to qualify your target audience or say no if they ask for something outside of your value offering has the potential to help you attract the right career or business as well as save you the time, energy and stress of the wrong opportunity.

Action 65: Re-attracting your existing target audience can be far more effective than starting with a new target audience for each and every career or business opportunity.

Section 10. Content Attraction Techniques

Action 66: There are many places where you can publish your own content or share content that you have curated, found, outsourced or interacted with. Sharing this content in the best locations for your target audience is a key to attracting the right career or business opportunity.

Action 67: There are some general principles for creating good quality evergreen and current content that will help you attract the right career or business and nourish your relationships. Be courageous and ready to share your story so that you can be found.

Action 68: Content is an excellent tool for attracting opportunities for your career or business but it needs to convert to be of real benefit. Make sure you include the essential ingredients so that your content does convert.

Action 69: Utilize various techniques to help your content reach your target audience through viral processes. Try to design your content and your sharing strategies so that they automatically trigger these processes without payment.

Action 70: Content that you write or help produce needs to be recorded, archived and shared to gain maximum attraction power. To secure lifetime value, add the details to your own website and to secure dynamic value, share it through other broadcast channels and individuals.

Action 71: Overcoming your own internal critical voice or someone else's criticism is not always easy but several strategies can be used to help you grow and develop from the experience.

Section 11. People Attraction Techniques

Action 72: To attract the right career or business opportunity, you need to think about what sort of people could help you on your journey. You also need to establish some selection criteria so that you can adopt a more targeted approach when sourcing these people.

Action 73: Do some background research on the key people in your career or business field that have been successful and find out what their 'secrets to success' have been. This will help you determine the types of people you need to find to assist you on your journey.

Action 74: Put on a smile and get out and about both online and offline to meet people that can help you on your journey to attracting the right career or business.

Action 75: After finding the people who can help you move to the next level, reach out to them, preferably by telephone and ask them questions to find the information you need. If you would like to maintain the relationship, find ways to keep in touch at least three times a year and automate and personalize the process.

Action 76: As your personal network grows and opportunities appear, you need to be able to review each career or business opportunity objectively and make good quality decisions. Ultimately, you will need to align your decisions with your values and purpose. Ideally, you will also build trusted relationships along the way.

Section 12. Platform Attraction Techniques

Action 77: Carefully assess the types of platforms that you can use for your values and purpose. Consider all of the variables before joining and make a reasonable effort to maintain your presence after joining. Be willing to close your account if it no longer serves your purpose.

Action 78: Complete each chosen Platform Profile for your purpose but be consistent, be careful (so that you don't accidentally choose the wrong options) and add the full list of platforms to your Google+ Profile in the Links section.

Action 79: Each platform has unique features and benefits that you can utilize for your purpose. Make sure your activity is aligned with the career or business opportunities you wish to attract and consider hiring a platform specialist to identify additional specific strategies that will maximize your attraction capacity.

Action 80: Measuring and monitoring your platform performance can help you work out what works and is worth pursuing and what doesn't work and needs to be reconsidered.

Action 81: Every platform or tool will have a range of features that will either help you attract the right career or business or keep you distracted from attracting the right career or business. Be discerning and see if you can find an experienced user to show you the best features for your purpose.

Action 82: Be aware that at any point in the future, there could be a significant change in the way that careers develop or businesses operate. By developing a networking strategy and multiple resource hubs, you have a greater ability to attract the right career or business and adjust to any changes in the marketplace.

Section 13. Process Attraction Techniques

Action 83: Process attraction techniques will help you continually find, select and complete activities that lead to new opportunities.

Action 84: Look beyond traditional career or business advertisement listings and find new locations for the potential career or business opportunity you are seeking.

Action 85: When applying for a career or business opportunity, make sure that you include all of the information that has been requested in a format that is matched to the decision maker's needs. Be consistent and persistent in your approach and don't make excuses if something you have tried does not work.

Action 86: Always do your best in interviews and meetings, but do not stress about the reasons why you may have missed out on the career or business opportunity. Simply relax and keep moving forward and do what you need to do to maintain your resilience, consistence and persistence.

Action 87: Start every career or business opportunity with an attitude of learning and understanding and start keeping records so that you can use this information in the future for your next steps.

Action 88: Find ways every day to live according to your values and purpose, even if your current situation is not completely aligned. Take action steps to develop the foundation for your future and be content with what you have achieved right now.

Action 89: To attract the right career or business opportunity, you need to be a lifelong learner. There are many free and low cost ways to learn new information and skills and it is never too late to start learning.

Action 90: There are many ways that you can be proactive both online and offline to generate signals to your target audience that you are interested in a career or business opportunity. You need to adopt a multi-channel, multi-media approach using multiple concurrent strategies and select the best options for your purpose.

Action 91: Although establishing a system based strategy for attracting career or business opportunities may take some initial time to set up, the potential rewards can be greater. Select the systems that will add the most value to your career or business goals.

Section 14. Possibility Attraction Techniques

Action 92: When you are presented with a possibility, take a moment to investigate your options and consider the opportunity. Be willing to take action based on research, probability and an appropriate risk assessment.

Action 93: To attract more possibilities in your career or business, increase your personal awareness of what is going on around you, be inquisitive and willing to explore new horizons.

Action 94: Explore how new systems and processes are creating possibilities to be found or work collaboratively, particularly if they involve you trialling and testing a new career or business opportunity before full implementation.

Action 95: Be prepared to put yourself out there for a zero initial return, particularly if it puts your details in front of your key target audience.

Action 96: Assess which possibility sources work best for you and your career or business and maintain them over time, but still be willing to modify your selection in the future as your goals change.

Section 15. Brand Development

Action 97: Brand Development involves selecting and implementing the best techniques for reminding people of your value. There are some things you cannot control. You must always be willing to apologize if things go wrong.

Action 98: Understand that everything you do and say both online and offline is part of your personal brand. Always strive to display good manners, etiquette and respect for local customs and say thank you whenever possible.

Action 99: Building a business brand that resonates with your specific target audience is a fantastic business attraction strategy.

Action 100: There are many different ways to build a personal brand online. Select the most useful for your target audience and one or two that are well recognized (like LinkedIn and Google My Business) to ensure that you appear in internet search results.

Action 101: Ratings, reviews, recommendations, testimonials, directory listings, industry specific listings, fans, celebrities, endorsements and expert status can all attract your target audience to your business.

Action 102: If you would like to secure some free publicity, it is a good idea to start with local publications so that you can build up your experience and resources for the time when a larger media outlet requests information.

Section 16. Network Development

Action 103: The degrees of separation between people are shrinking and thanks to technology, building an extensive network has become easier.

Action 104: Visit a networking group at least twice before joining the group and make sure that they pass your network assessment criteria before you make a regular commitment. Remember that networking involves giving and receiving. If you can't find a network that fits your purpose, consider creating one.

Action 105: Creating a network requires commitment, but with a good networking group model, you can design a network that will help you achieve your purpose.

Action 106: If you plan to network, learn the best tips and techniques for effective networking so that you can attract the right career or business opportunities.

Action 107: Design your own personal system for managing the new people you meet so that you can build your network over time and manage the VIPs for your purpose.

Action 108: By valuing your network and the relationships with your network members, you will become a magnet for the right career and business opportunities.

Section 17. Website Development

Action 109: Remember that a website is never finished and must constantly be updated and evolved over time.

Action 110: A personal career attraction website provides a lifetime value record of your career and allows you to attract future career opportunities. You can choose a free WordPress.com site that can be exported at a later date or start with your own domain name website with personally purchased website hosting and WordPress.org as your website design platform.

Action 111: A personal business attraction website allows you to attract business career opportunities directly. When you start, you can either use it as a one stop shop or in conjunction with a freelancer portal or shopping service.

Action 112: Every website that is published should be connected to Google, have backup, security, caching and SEO features installed, load quickly, be mobile friendly, have new content added regularly, be connected to social media and be added to relevant directory listings.

Action 113: Make sure that you understand the basic performance measures of your website and how to see these results via your Google Analytics account.

Action 114: Seek input from other people and your target audience about how your website works from their perspective and then consider making changes in conjunction with your website designer.

Section 18. Overcoming Challenges

Action 115: On your journey to attracting the right career or business opportunities, you will face challenges. Don't stop. Keep taking action and be persistent and when you look back, you will see how far you have come.

Action 116: Planning the various actions that you will complete in date order with realistic time frames will help you achieve your goals. Remember to review what works and keep a record of your wins and losses so that you can celebrate your achievements and plan your next action steps.

Action 117: By measuring your results along your career or business attraction journey, you will see how the actions you are taking are helping you reach your destination. Don't stop. Keep going.

Action 118: Think about what personal blockages you might be carrying with you right now and think about one thing you could do today that is slightly different from yesterday. See if you can repeat it tomorrow as well and have a look in a year's time and see what is different about your life.

Action 119: Understand that sometimes in life, you cannot change the external environment, you can only adapt to the external environment. Find out what you can re-use, how you can maintain your consistency and persistence and be extremely grateful for everything you have right now.

Action 120: Review the Top 20 Tips and Techniques and make an effort to complete at least one of these in the next month.

20. Bonuses

To access the free Special Bonus Offers from this book, you will need to join the 120 Ways Publishing Membership Program at http://120ways.com/members

You can select the free Personal Membership Program or consider an Upgrade to the Professional or Premium Membership Program.

The free Special Downloads that you will automatically have access to in the Personal Membership Program include:

1. Excel Spreadsheet file for you to record the details of all of your **Usernames and Passwords** for all of your accounts

2. Excel Spreadsheet file of all of the **Links** mentioned in this book

3. **Suggested Resume / CV Template** layout for you to consider as a pro-forma for creating a file that is suitable for an Applicant Tracking System (ATS)

4. Suggested **Business Introduction Template** layout for you to consider if you would like to contact local businesss for a suitable position

120 Ways Publishing Membership Program - Valid for ALL Books!			
Correct as at 24 May 2016	Personal	Professional	Premium
Free Email News (Value $100)	√	√	√
Free Lifetime Access to Later Edition Summaries (Value $250)	√	√	√
Free Lifetime Access to Special Download Files offered in the books (Value $150)	√	√	√
Access to Questions & Answers Summaries (Value $500)		√	√
Access to How-To Instruction Videos and Audio Recordings (Value $1,500)			√
Total Value	$500	$1,000	$2,500
Investment	Free	$39 a year*	$59 a year*

The pricing for the Professional and Premium membership levels may change in the future but we will always do our best to keep these as affordable as possible and still provide maximum value.

The best part of the 120 Ways Publishing Membership Program is that if you become a member, you will also have access to all of the other equivalent products from our other books!

Upcoming Book: 120 Ways To Market Your Business Hyper Locally

Previous Book: 120 Ways To Achieve Your Purpose With LinkedIn

Join the 120 Ways Publishing Membership Program right now at

http://120ways.com/members

Index

This index was manually created to give you direct access to many important topics in this book. If you have a digital version of this book, you can also search for topics by keyword.

The index quotes Section Numbers rather than Page Numbers.

120 Ways Publishing 9.3
A/B testing 17.4
ability 5.5
accepting a job offer 7.10
account manage 7.7
account management matrix 13.7
accountability partner 1.2, 5.6, 11
achievements 1, 15.3
action 13.3
action plan 18.2
action planning 18.1
action steps 1.2, 6
action to attraction 1
ad blocking software 12.5
adventure 14.1
advertised opportunities 13.1, 13.2
advertisements 10.2, 13.1
advertising 8.3
advertorial 10.2
advocate 15.3agents 15.5
aggregator sites 12.5
aggregator sites 13.1
algorithims 2.1, 6.4, 8.5, 10.3, 10.4, 12.2, 13.7, 14.2
Alibaba 17.2
aligned job 7.3
alumni 7.4
Amazon 17.2
ambassador 15.3
ambition 2.6
analysis paralysis 6.4
anecdotes 1, 2.3, 4.1
anxiety 2.2
apology 15
Applicant Tracking Systems (ATS) 13.2
apprenticeship 13.6
apps 2.1, 10, 12.4, 13.8
archive.org 10.1, 10.4, 13.7

artificial intelligence 2.1, 12.5
assess 6.2
assessing networks 16.1
assessment 8.1
asset value in business 8.9
assumptions 1
attention economy 2.1
audience attraction techniques 9
audience locations 9.1
authentic 7.8, 14.4
authenticity 2.2
authenticity 16.5
authority websites 17.2
automation 13.8
avatar 12.1
avoid 3

B2B 9
B2C 9
backup 17.3
bad behaviors 5.8
bad reviews 10.5
bargain hunters 8.7
best content 10
blessing 13.5
blog 6.1, 17.2
bloggers 15.4
Bluehost 17.1
body language 13.3
book 14.2, 14.3
books 2.6
bounce rate 17.4
boundaries 2.7
brain 2.2, 5.2, 7.4, 8.3
brains or brawn 2.6
brand awareness 2
brand development 15
brave 10.5
bribes 13.4
budget 5.4
bulk content 10
business brand 15.2, 15.4
business demand 8.4
business disruption 8.5
business margin 2.4

business mentor 11.4
business models 8.7
business performance 8.7
business with people 8.3
buyer beware 12.1

caching 17.3
calculated risks 1.3
call to action 10.2
Camberwell Network 16.4
capital raising 5
career anchors 7
career counselling 3
career development 3
career pathways 2
cash flow 8.1
celebrate 2.2, 6.7
centers of influence 16.4
certainty 2.5
certification 13.6, 13.8
challenge 2.5
challenges 5.5, 6.8, 10.5, 18
champion 15.3
children 5.6
choosing the right career introduction
circulation numbers 10.3
clarity introduction, 1, 3, 8.6,
clarity value in business 8.4
click bait 10.2
click conversions 10.2
cloud 12.3
clutter 18.2
coaching 12.2
cognitive computing 2.1
collaboration 14.2
collective 14.2
collective unconcious 2
collectivist culture 2.7
comfort zone 2.6, 10.5, 13.5
commitment 2.2, 5.6
communications 15.5
competitor analysis 17.3
competitors 8.5
complaints 5.7
conciously incompetent 13.4

confidential information 7.8
connectifier 11.3
conscious choices 6.8
consequences 12.2, 14.2
consiously competent 13.4
consistency 13.2, 15.5
content 2.6, 10, 10.4
content archive 12
content bank 10.3
content critics 10.5
content distribution 10.3
content locations 10
content marketing 10.3
content reach 10.3
contentment 13.5
contracting 13.1
control 2.1, 4
conversational content 10.1
conversion 8.3
conversions 10.2, 17.4
creating a network 16.2
credibility 2.2, 5.7, 9.1, 14.4, 15.4
credibility capital 5.7
crisis introduction
criticism 7.8, 10.5, 15.1
crowdfund 2.1
crowdsource 2.1
crystalized time 5.4
crystalknows 11.3
cultural capital 5.3
cultural fit 13.3
cultural intelligence 2.6
culturally competent 5.3
culture 13.7
curate 10
customer experience 2, 2.1, 17.4
customer-ization 13.8
customs 15.1
CVs 13.2
cycle of life 6.8

data 2.1, 4.1, 8.10
data analytics 17.4
data science 2.1
database 14.3

databases 14.2
decision maker 13.3
decision makers 7.8, 8.10, 9.1, 12.3, 13.2, 15.5
decision making 8.6, 11.4, 13.7, 14
decisions 4.1
declutter 1.2
demand economy 2.1
depression 2.2
developing your network 16.4
dicipline 2.2
difference 5.3
digital assets 8.9
digital disruption 8.6
digital era 8.6
digital executor 2.1
digital literacy 2
digital literacy 8.8, 8.9
direct message 10.4
directory listings 15.4
diversity 13.5
domain name 6.1, 12, 17.1
domestic violence 5.6
dot points 7.6
due dilligence 4.1
dynamic value 6.4, 8.9, 12.5, 13.7

eBay 17.2
e-commerce 17.2
education 2.6
education 5.2, 5.4, 6.7, 13.6
email 17.1
email newsletter 13.7
emotional intelligence 2.6
encouragement 7.7
entrepreneur 7.4, 8.9
ethics 13.5
etiquette 15.1, 16.5
Etsy 17.2
events 13.8, 14.3, 16.2
evergreen content 10.1
everything for free 12.5
exhange relationship 16.3
exit strategy 8.9
experts 9.1, 10.1, 11.1
external blockages 18.4

extrinsic needs 2.5
extroverts 11
Facebook 6.5, 9.1, 10.3, 11.3, 12.3, 12.4, 13.1
Facebook advertisement 6.5
fair exchange 1, 1.1, 2.4, 8.7
faith or religious group 13.7
family 5.4
family of origin 3
feedback 2, 6.3, 6.6, 7.7, 7.9, 12.3, 13.7, 15.1
financial capital 5.4
financial wealth 2.4
find a job 7.5
first person 7.6
fishing 2.1
Fiverr 17.2
fixed assets 8.9
flow 2.2, 2.3
foggy brain 1.2
follow up 6.6, 7.9, 11.2
formatting 7.6
forums 12.4
foundation 13.5
foundations 18.1
framework 3
framework for decisions 2.7
free lunch 9.2
freelance 14.2
Freelancer 17.2
freelancing 13.1
freemium 12.2
friends 11
Full Page Screen Capture 12.3
fun food and free 13.4
future context 2.1

game changers 2.1, 12.5
get rich quick schemes 1.1
gifts 7.9, 13.5
gig economy 2.1
give 2
givers gain 16.1
global warming 6.8
goals 1, 1.2, 2.2, 6, 6.2
good lunch 9.2
Google + local 12.4

Google Account 17.1, 17.3
Google Alert 8.5, 17.3
Google Analytics 17.3
Google Analytics 17.4
Google chrome extension 12.3
Google Maps 12.4
Google My Business 12.4, 15.3
Google My Business 15.3
Google Places 12.4
Google Plus 12.4, 17.1
Google Profile 12.1
Google Search Console 17.3
governance 13.4
government initiatives 14.1
grapevine 14.1
gratefulness 5.5
gratitude introduction
gratitude 18.4
gratitude capital 5.5, 6.6
gravatar 12.1
Greek fisherman 5.4
group success 2.7
grow organically 8.9
guest speaker 14.3
guest speaking 16.1
guru 15.3
gut 2.6, 11.1

handle 10.4
happiness trap 13.5
harmonious society 13.5
hashtags 10.4, 12.
head 8.6
head hunters 7
headline 15.5
heart 2.6, 8.6
helplessness 4.1
high authority website 10.3
high moral ground 15.1
homework 6.1
human interest story 15.5
human resources 8.8
human tribes 11
human value in business 8.8
hypnotherapist 2.3

hypnotic language 10.1

images 10.2
immediate job 7.1
implementation 2.6
individualistic culture 2.7
induction 13.4
industry died 18.4
industry initiatives 14.1
industry listings 15.4
influence capital 5.8
influencer 15.3
influences 10.1
informal education 13.6
informal training 1.3
inside information 13.2
Instagram 12.3, 12.4
instant gratification 1
instinct 2.6
intellectual capital 5.2
intellectual intelligence 2.6
intention 16.3
interact with content 10
internet search results 6.3, 10.4, 11.3, 12.1
internship 16.5
interview clothing 7.8
interview techniques 7.8
intrinsic needs 2.5
introverts 11
investment 8.10
investment strategy 8.10
investment value in business 8.10
investors 8.10

jargon 7.6
job advertisements 7.5, 14.2
job aggregator websites 7.5
job application 13.2, 13.3
job applications 7.6
job interview 13.3
job interviews 7.8
journalists 10, 15.5

keywords 7.6, 17.3
knots 1.3

knots 6.5
knowledge economy 2.1

landing pages 7.5
language literacy 8.8
leadership 5.8
learners 13.6
learning 2, 8.8, 10.5
learning junkie 1.3
let go 11.3
letting go 1.4, 2, 2.3, 18.1
leverage 2.4
lifestyle 5.4, 5.5, 18.4
lifetime value 6.4, 8.9, 12.5, 13.7, 17.1
limiting beliefs 2.5, 18.3
Linked In 15.3
LinkedIn 6.1, 6.3, 8.4, 8.5, 8.9, 9.3, 10.1, 11.3, 12.2, 12.4, 17.1
links 12.1
local laws 7.8
local shopping 8.4
location 10.3, 11
logical and psychological adjustment 2.6
logos 6.2
lone ranger 13.7
loyalty 2.6, 5.6
luck 1

maintenance 6.2, 6.4, 14.4
making decisions 2.7, 6.8, 17.4, 18.3
management skills 7.3
manager 5.8
managers 2.5
manifestation 7.7
manners 15.1
market conditions 3
market forces 18.4
market place 8.3
marketing 13.7, 13.8, 14.2
marketing funnel 8.3
mass manipulation 12.5
mass sackings 8.8
means to an end job 7.2
measuring results 18.2
media 15.3, 15.5
media publicity 10

meetings 11.3
memberships 13.8
mentoring 13.6
mentors 11.2
migrants 2.7
mindmap 3
mindset 2.2
minimum viable product 4.1
missionary 15.3
mistakes 11.1
mobile friendly website 17.3
money 5.4
monocultural 5.3
motivation to change 18.3
move 4, 4.1, 5.3, 7.8
movers and shakers 14.3
moving 2.6
multicultural 5.3
multiple concurrent strategies 1, 6.4, 7.5, 7.7, 9.1

nature versus nurture introduction
negative affirmations 18.3
negative message 15.1
neighbors 14.3
network criteria 16.1
network development 16
network is your net worth 16.5
network value 16.5
networking 12.5, 16.2
networking etiquette 16.3
networking group model 16.2
networking system 16.4
new ideas 11.1
new job 7.10
new normal 2
Newcomers Network 6.7, 10, 15.2, 16, 16.4
next step up jobs 7.4
nina4airbnb 13.7
non cognitive skills 2
non negotiables 3
non target audience 9.3
no-shows 16.2

offline profile 6.2
okay for now job 9.3

old age 2.2
old school 8.5
onboarding 13.4
one source of truth 16.4
online forums 7.5
online platform 12
online platforms 6.5, 7.6, 10.3
online profile 6.2, 12.1
online traders 8.3
operating capital 5.5
outcomes 18.2
outsource 2.1
outsource content 10
outsourcing 13.1
overcoming challenges 7.3
overcoming fear 6.7
overnight success 11.1
own website 6.1
ownership 6.4

pages per visit 17.4
paralysed by fear 10.5
parenting skills 5.6
partnerships 11
past 3
past behavior 7
paternalistic 15.1
pay to play 12.2
paying it forward 11.4
peace 13.5
people aggregator 11.3
perceived value 12.5
perceived value in business 8.2
perception 15
performance 2.6, 12.3
perseverence introduction, 3
persistence 1, 7.4, 7.7, 13.2, 15.5
personal blockages 18.3
personal brand 15.1, 15.3
personal business attraction website 17.2
personal career attraction website 17.1
personal development 14.1
personal identity 2.1
personal needs 14.4
personal responsibility 1.1

personality preferences 13.3
personalization 2.1, 9.3, 12.5
personnel 8.8
phone interview 7.8
photos 6.2
physical health 2.4
Pinterest 12.3, 12.4
plan B 6.1
planning 4.1
plateau 11.3
positive affirmations 18.3
possibility 14, 14.1, 14.2, 14.3, 14.4
potential 2.6
PR 15.5
pre selling 9.2
predictive artificial intelligence 12.5
predictive intelligence 2.1
pricing value in business 8.7
privacy 2.1
privacy by choice 2.1
pro bono work 11.4
proactive 13.7
probability 14
problem solving 15.5
process attraction strategies 13
procrastination 1.2, 11.1, 18
product-ization 13.8
professional assistance introduction
professional help 1.4, 2, 2.3, 13.5, 18.1
professional reputation 4.1
profit margin 8.7, 13.8
profit versus purpose 1
promotion 4, 9.3, 15.5
protirement 2
public relations 8.2, 15.5
publicity 15.5
publicity campaign 15.5
purpose 2.2, 2.5, 2.6, 3, 5.4, 7.2

qualification 13.6
quality content 10.1, 10.2
quality real estate 6.2, 8.2
quick wins 18.1

ratings 8.2, 15.4
raving fans 15.4
real estate 18.1
real value 8.1
realistic 7.10
realistic 8.1
receive 1.1, 2
reciprocity value in business 8.5
recognition 2.5
recognition 2.7
recommendations 5.7, 15.4
records 6.1
recruitment 3, 7, 7.5, 9.2
referral value in business 8.3
referrals 7, 8.3, 11.3, 13.2, 13.7, 16.5
refferal economy 2.1
regret 18
relationship 15.2
relationship capital 5.6
relationship management 16.4
relationships 2.3, 5.6, 6.6, 11.3
relaxation 18.1
relevant 7.6
reliability 9.1
reputation 7.9, 15.4
reputation economy 2.1
research 3, 6.1, 7.1, 7.6, 11.1, 11.3, 14.2
resiliance 18
resource hubs 12.5
resources 13.8
responsibility 2.2, 2.6
responsive design 17.3
results 18.1
resumes 13.2
retailers 8.5
retention 7
retirement 2
return on investment 6.4
reviews 8.2, 10.5, 15.4
reward 2.5, 2.7
Richard Branson 8.6
risk 2.4, 4.1, 7, 10.4, 11, 14
risk assessment 12
risk mitigation strategy 8.2
rleonardi 13.7

robots 8.8

sabotage 2.2, 2.3, 2.5
safety 13.4
savings 5.4
say thank you 3
scalable 13.8
scale 2.4
scannable 7.6
screenshots 12.3
search engine optimization 12.1, 15.3
search results 6.3
seasons 6.8
secret operations 8.5
security 17.3
security settings 7.6, 12.2
seeds 13.8
selection criteria 11
self directed learning 13.6
self discipline 1
self image 2.6
self sabotage 18
SEO 17.3
share content 10
share the love 8.5
sharing economy 2.1, 14.2
sharpen the saw 1.4
shiny object syndrome 7.4, 8.1, 12.4
shopping service 17.2
sideways 4
silver bullet 1.1, 1.3
simplicity 2.5
site map 17.4
site speed 17.4
six degrees of separation 16
skills 4
skills intelligence 2.6
small business 15.2
smile 6.6, 11.2, 13.3
SMS 12.4
social capital 5.1
social economy 2.1
social entrepeneur 5.1
social justice 8.5

social media 7.5, 8.2, 9.3, 10.2, 10.4, 11.3, 13.7, 14.2, 15.4
specialize 5.8
speculative 8.10
speed 9.2
spider's web 7.5, 10.4
standards 5.8
start at the bottom introduction
startups 1.3
statistics 12.3, 15.3, 18.2
stock photos 17.3
stomach 8.6
story 10.1, 10.5, 15.5
strengths 3
success 2.4, 5.4
suppliers 8.5
survival job 7.2
survival mode 6.7
survive 5.4
sustainable business 8.9
synchronicity 2, 2.5
systems 18.2

tag exchange 10.3
tagging 10.4
talent 15.5
talent created roles 7.5
target audience 8.1, 8.3, 9, 9.2, 9.3, 10.4, 11.2, 12.5, 13.8, 15.2, 15.4, 15.5, 18, 18.1
teaching 5.2, 14.3
team size 7.4
technical skills 7.3
technology 13.7
tender 14.3
test 6.2
test and tell tools 3
testimonials 15.4
text does not give context 10.1
thank you 6.6, 7.5, 7.9, 11.2
third person 7.6
thought leader 15.3
thought leaders 10.1, 11.1
tire kickers 9.3
to-do lists 1.2
to-do schedule 1.2
trade 13.6
transferable skills 6.1, 18.4

triggers 2
trust 2, 2.2, 2.6, 11.3, 11.4
Twitter 10.3, 12.2, 12.4
two hours per day five days per week 1.4

uncertainty 2.5
uncertainty value in business 8.6
unconciously competent 13.4
unconciously incompetent 13.4
unconscious bias 18.4
unique content 10.1
unique selling p roposition 2.6
upsells 8.3
Upwork 17.2
usability 17.4
user experience 17.4
usernames and passwords list 12, 18.1, 18.2

value 8
value yourself 2.4
values 2.5, 3, 5.4, 5.5, 5.6, 7.2
vanity metrics 10.2
vanity results 2.1, 10.3
variety 2.5
venture capitalist 1.3
very important person (VIP) 16.4
victim 1.2
video 7.5
view page source 17.3
viral 10.3
virtual interview 7.8
vision 2.2, 13.5
vocational courses 13.6
voluntary work 3, 5.1, 8.5, 13.2, 13.7, 14.2
volunteering 13.6

walking on egg shells 2.7
weaknesses 3
wearable technology 2.1, 12.4
webinars 13.8
website 6.4, 8.9, 10, 11.3, 12
website development 17, 17.3
website feedback 17.4
website hosting 17.1
website performance measures 17.4

wheel hub 13.8
white label 8.5
wholesalers 8.5
wilderness 1.2
wins 1
wins and losses 18.1
wisdom 6.8
WordPress 6.1, 6.4, 10.3
WordPress.com 17.1
WordPress.org 17.1
work ethic introduction
work experience 13.7
work life balance 14.2
working to live 2
workplace 13.4
worst thing 8.6
worth 8.7
worth you attract 2.4

Yammer 12.4

Author

Sue Ellson BBus AIMM MAHRI CDAA (Assoc) ASA MPC

Sue Ellson is an experienced trainer, professional learner, consultant in practice and an Independent LinkedIn Specialist.

Sue was born in Adelaide, South Australia in 1965. Sue was married in 1985 and moved to Melbourne in Victoria, Australia in 1994. She had two children in 1995 and 1997 and was granted a divorce in 2006. Sue enjoys the simple pleasures of life – like being able to walk and breathing fresh air.

Sue has completed a Bachelor of Business in Administrative Management from the University of South Australia (2000) http://unisa.edu.au, is a Member of the Australian Institute of Management AIM (since 2001) http://aim.com.au, a Member of the Australian Human Resources Institute AHRI (since 2005) http://ahri.com.au, a Member of the Melbourne Press Club (since 2008) http://melbournepressclub.com, an Associate Member of the Career Development Association of Australia CDAA (since 2015) http://cdaa.org.au and a Member of the Australian Society of Authors ASA (since 2015) http://asauthors.org.

Sue has a varied range of professional experience in banking, training, recruitment, career development, human resources, marketing, networking, online publishing, social media and business. Sue's first enterprise, Newcomers Network was started in 1999 and her first website http://newcomersnetwork.com went live in 2001.Newcomers Network and Sue's close circle of local and international friends have helped her understand the needs of people from many different cultures and countries.

Sue joined LinkedIn on 21 December 2003. Sue has been consulting, training, speaking, writing and advising on the topic of LinkedIn since 2008. In 2012, she created Camberwell Network http://camberwellnetwork.com and in 2015, she created 120 Ways Publishing http://120ways.com.

More information about Sue is online at http://sueellson.com. LinkedIn connections are welcome at http://au.linkedin.com/in/sueellson

Google reviews are very welcome at https://plus.google.com/+Sueellson2

Sue Ellson - Topics

Sue knows how to gather information on a variety of topics, but is most passionate about:
> helping people achieve their purpose (career or business)
> utilizing LinkedIn and technology to achieve a purpose
> the successful settlement of newcomers, expatriates and repatriates
> the value of local communities and becoming more connected

Sue Ellson - Speaking and Training

Sue welcomes selected opportunities to be a keynote speaker, guest presenter, trainer or webinar guest at conferences, seminars and professional development events in Australia and overseas. Her previous presentations are listed at http://sueellson.com/presentations

Sue Ellson - Consulting

Sue provides personally tailored individual and group consulting services in Melbourne and via Skype, or with sufficient notice, in person elsewhere depending on availability. Her current services are listed at http://sueellson.com/services

Sue Ellson - Publications

Sue has written a variety of articles for many different publications and welcomes selected opportunities to provide exclusive written content. Her previous publications are listed at http://sueellson.com/publications

Sue Ellson - Media Requests

Sue has provided a range of content to newspapers, magazines and online publications and has been a guest on radio programs both in Australia and overseas. More information at http://sueellson.com/about

To Contact Sue Ellson

sueellson@sueellson.com
http://sueellson.com
http://120ways.com
http://newcomersnetwork.com
http://camberwellnetwork.com
http://au.linkedin.com/in/sueellson

Copyright

All text and technical diagrams copyright © Sue Ellson 2016. The moral rights of the author have been asserted. All rights reserved.

Photocopying and reproducing in print or digital format

If recommending the content in this book to friends, family, clients or colleagues, please keep in mind that the original rights belong to the author only.

The content has been generously provided and it is only fair that the reward be returned to the author to recover the cost of production, distribution and future editions. If you wish to reproduce, store or transmit any part of this book, please email the publisher 120ways@120ways.com for written permission rights. All quotations need to be referenced to Sue Ellson

---

Join the 120 Ways Publishing Membership Program NOW!

For free bonuses valued at $500
http://120ways.com/members

www.ingramcontent.com/pod-product-compliance
Lightning Source LLC
Chambersburg PA
CBHW070557300426
44113CB00010B/1292